RAND PROJECT AIR FORCE

The Nevada Test and Training Range (NTTR) and Proposed Wilderness Areas

Issues Affecting the NTTR's Land Withdrawal Renewal

Beth E. Lachman, John A. Ausink, William A. Williams, Katherine Pfrommer, Manuel J. Carrillo

Prepared for the United States Air Force
Approved for public release; distribution unlimited

For more information on this publication, visit www.rand.org/t/RR1105

Library of Congress Cataloging-in-Publication Data is available for this publication.
ISBN: 978-0-8330-9237-3

Published by the RAND Corporation, Santa Monica, Calif.

Preface

This research seeks to help the U.S. Air Force (USAF) understand broad strategic issues related to the future purpose and use of the withdrawn lands that make up the Nevada Test and Training Range (NTTR). One strategic issue relates to restrictions that the USAF and the U.S. Fish and Wildlife Service (USFWS) are observing in proposed wilderness areas that are located in land co-managed by the NTTR and the Desert National Wildlife Range (DNWR), the largest national wildlife refuge outside of Alaska. These restrictions complicate operational practices for the USAF test and training activity being conducted on these lands. We found that the USAF has a range of options for working with the USFWS to acquire more operational flexibility on shared NTTR and DNWR lands.

This document is intended to help senior leaders better understand how these USAF-managed lands came to be restricted by the wilderness proposal. It characterizes the historical use of the land, describes how USAF range operational practices are being constrained, and discusses options to improve USAF operations on the DNWR portion of the NTTR, regardless of whether Congress approves the wilderness proposal. The ultimate goal is to inform test and training enterprise decisions and help the USAF and the USFWS improve the management of these withdrawn lands, given both their purposes and needs.

This document is one of a series of research documents to better equip senior leaders in the Air Force, the Department of Defense (DoD) and Department of the Interior (DOI) who are working with Congress when setting priorities for the withdrawn lands and other NTTR resources.

The research reported here was commissioned by the Air Force Civil Engineer Center and conducted within the Manpower, Personnel, and Training Program of RAND Project AIR FORCE as part of a fiscal year 2014 project, "Nevada Test and Training Range (NTTR) Renewal: A Strategic Look."

RAND Project AIR FORCE

RAND Project AIR FORCE (PAF), a division of the RAND Corporation, is the U.S. Air Force's federally funded research and development center for studies and analyses. PAF provides the Air Force with independent analyses of policy alternatives affecting the development, employment, combat readiness, and support of current and future air, space, and cyber forces. Research is conducted in four programs: Force Modernization and Employment; Manpower, Personnel, and Training; Resource Management; and Strategy and Doctrine. The research reported here was prepared under contract FA7014-06-C-0001.

Additional information about PAF is available on our website:

http://www.rand.org/paf/

This report documents work originally shared with the U.S. Air Force on August 5, 2014. The draft report, issued on September 16, 2014, was reviewed by formal peer reviewers and U.S. Air Force subject-matter experts.

Contents

Figures

Tables

Summary

The Nevada Test and Training Range (NTTR), located in southern Nevada, is the only location in the United States where full-scale battlefield scenarios can be simulated for individual and multi-force training. The testing and training available at the NTTR is "crucial to the survival" of U.S. military personnel and to the success of their missions.[1] As a Major Range and Test Facility Base (MRTFB), the NTTR also is a core element of Department of Defense (DoD) Test and Evaluation (T&E) infrastructure and must be preserved as a national asset.

Land can be withdrawn, or removed, from public use and reserved for military training and testing in support of national defense requirements. The most recent withdrawal of the 2.9 million acres of land in the NTTR was authorized in October 1999 by Title XXX of Public Law 106-65, the National Defense Authorization Act for Fiscal Year 2000. This authorization expires November 6, 2021, and to renew the land withdrawal, the Air Force must submit a request to the Bureau of Land Management (BLM). In preparation for the development of the request, the Air Force asked RAND's Project Air Force to help it review the broad strategic issues related to the future purpose and use of the withdrawn lands that make up the NTTR.[2]

One of these issues is that the southeastern part of the NTTR overlaps the Desert National Wildlife Range (DNWR), which is just north of the Las Vegas metropolitan area. The overlapping area is co-managed by the Air Force and the U.S. Fish and Wildlife Service (USFWS), which, like the BLM, is housed in the Department of the Interior (DOI). Since 1974, a significant part of the overlapping lands has been designated as "proposed wilderness," which means that the lands must be protected as *de facto* wilderness, even though Congress has not acted on the wilderness proposal. This status—and the uncertainty about what Congress might do with the proposal—restricts how the Air Force can use the land and the airspace above it in its training, testing, and other operations, as well as what kinds of activities it can undertake in managing the land. For example, it imposes some limits on ground operations and the placement or relocation of targets and threats. It also shapes USFWS' approach to active wildlife and land management. However, even if Congress rejected the proposed wilderness on the DNWR or the wilderness proposal was withdrawn, the USAF still would find it difficult to make any significant changes in its operations on the DNWR if they would affect the lands and environment.

---

[1] Nellis Air Force Base, *Final Integrated Natural Resources Management Plan, Nellis Air Force Base/Creech Air Force Base/Nevada Test and Training Range*, Nellis Air Force Base, Nev.: 99th Civil Engineering Squadron, Environmental Management Flight, February 2010, p. 8.

[2] The purpose and use of lands that make up the NTTR are addressed in Ausink et al., *The Nevada Test and Training Range (NTTR): Purpose and Need for Renewing the Withdrawal of Lands from Public Use*, RR-1035-AF.

This document provides background on the proposed wilderness designation; the limits that it places on Air Force training; and potential approaches to mitigating these limits that decision-makers should consider as part of, and even separately from, a strategy related to the renewal of the land-withdrawal authorization.

The Air Force has several options for obtaining greater operational flexibility in the NTTR areas that are proposed as wilderness. All of these options would require working with the USFWS, and within official USFWS processes, to meet Air Force objectives. Several of these already have been under way at the local level for some time:

1. Headquarters USAF could explore with DOI and USFWS the possibility of withdrawing the wilderness proposal for the part of the DNWR lands that fall within the NTTR. This may require congressional action, as it is not uncommon for wilderness proposals to lie dormant for decades, and some proposals were submitted to congressional committees that no longer exist.
2. The Air Force could persuade the USFWS to take into account a greater share of USAF mission requirements in the agency's implementation of the DNWR comprehensive conservation plan. The management of refuges is supposed to fully consider the resource priorities and management strategies of other federal, state, and local organizations; this represents an opportunity for the Air Force to acquire some operational changes in the NTTR DNWR areas to meet Air Force management and mission needs. Addressing this important step may require the Office of the Assistant Secretary of the Air Force for Installations, Environment and Logistics (SAF/IEE) Regional Environmental Office in San Francisco to engage with the USFWS Regional Office Headquarters in Sacramento, or at the Washington D.C. headquarters level if contentious issues arise.[3]
3. As of July 2015 the Air Force and USFWS were working to revise the 1997 memorandum of understanding (MOU) that governs co-management of the DNWR lands within the NTTR. This may be a good opportunity to negotiate potential changes that allow more flexibility for Air Force operations. This is an ongoing process with NTTR, Nellis AFB and Air Combat Command (ACC) staff working with USFWS staff at the DNWR. Contentious issues may need to be raised to the AF and U.S. Fish and Wildlife Service headquarters level to help move the effort forward.
4. The USAF could approach the USFWS about conducting a minimum requirements analysis (MRA) for DNWR management activities that affect Air Force range management considerations, such as allowing the building of a new dirt road. The MRA process helps to create exceptions to land-use prohibitions for the purposes of managing

[3] From an Air Force perspective, it may seem that it is standard operating procedure to start at the local level and then elevate issues if necessary to improve communication. Those we interviewed often didn't know at what level to begin addressing the root causes of co-management problems.

wilderness lands. This request also may have to be initiated at the Office of the Assistant Secretary of the Air Force for Installations, Environment and Logistics (SAF/IE) level or higher if local NTTR staff requests for USFWS to conduct an official MRA for the DNWR are not acted on by the staff at the DNWR.

5. The Air Force could ask the USFWS to conduct a formal wilderness review process for the DNWR to see if DNWR lands in the NTTR are still suitable for wilderness designation. This option may be required procedurally, since the original proposal is now in Congress. The USAF could argue that the original wilderness proposal may not properly reflect the current conditions of DNWR lands, since it has been more than 40 years since the original wilderness proposal was assessed and proposed.[4]
6. The Air Force has been given "primary jurisdiction" of some impact areas within the DNWR. The Air Force could explore with the USFWS the possibility of transferring primary jurisdiction to the Air Force of additional areas that are considered crucial to the future mission activity of meeting national security requirements and the maintenance of testing and training capabilities. With transfer of primary jurisdiction and a carefully negotiated memorandum of understanding, it might be possible for the Air Force and the USFWS to satisfy, in large part, their sometimes conflicting goals. However, this option is likely to be expensive.

A crucial part of building a required strategy for any of these options is a clear and explicit purpose and needs statement in which the USAF articulates the enduring need for its withdrawn lands. It also is important to note that, because of the amount of land that the wilderness criteria currently protect, it is almost-certain that operational and support inefficiencies for NTTR operations would arise. Given congressional direction in 2012 for the Services to maximize the utility of their use public lands withdrawn for military use, especially in light of fiscal guidance, the USAF should use and manage NTTR lands efficiently. As this research effort began, DoD was deep into a Strategic Choices Management Review that scrutinized all aspects of DoD's budget.[5] Fiscal guidance from the Secretary of Defense continues to call for reductions in overhead and associated costs to preserve and strengthen military readiness—a primary objective for NTTR operations.[6]

The Air Force has a range of options to pursue for acquiring the required operational flexibility on NTTR DNWR proposed wilderness lands. By specifically identifying which operational activities they most want to improve, NTTR staff, ACC and Headquarters Air Force

---

[4] An indication of this is a new DNWR description of affected lands that was received by the NTTR and attempts to "correct" boundary issues.

[5] U.S. Department of Defense, "Department of Defense Press Briefing by Secretary Hagel and Adm. Winnefeld from the Pentagon," Office of the Assistant Secretary of Defense (Public Affairs), July 31, 2013, p. 1.

[6] U.S. Department of Defense, 2013, p. 2.

could pursue one or more of these options with USFWS staff and likely gain more operational flexibility on DNWR lands at NTTR to benefit the mission.

Acknowledgments

This report draws on RAND Project Air Force work reaching back to 2013 as a consequence of a broader project looking at renewing lands withdrawn from the BLM in 1940 for use as a gunnery range. It builds on a body of Airspace and Range Management research performed for the Air Force, Army, and the Office of the Secretary of Defense (OSD) since 2001. For this document, we are deeply indebted to the diverse group of subject-matter experts both those in DoD and in outside organizations who helped with the project. This work benefited immeasurably from their experience and insights into the "wilderness question" pertaining to Nevada Test and Training Range lands withdrawn for Air Force use.

We especially appreciated the insight and NTTR planning information from Mr. Roger Christensen and Lt Col Herman Schirg, NTTR/XP, and their help with arranging meetings in Southern Nevada with Air Force, and other local stakeholders. Mr. Danny Douglass, NTTR/DO helped provide NTTR operations data on airspace and land access.

We also thank the leadership and staff of the Air Force Civil Engineer Center, specifically Mr. Eldon Hix, AFCEC/CZ, who is our research project sponsor. We would like to single out Mr. Joseph P. Ebert, AFCEC/CIBW as the point man for AFCEC, and Mr. Jonathan Haliscak and Ms Joan Kuecker, AFCEC/CZTQ, for their patient assistance. Mr. Michael Ackerman and Captain David Murley of AFCEC/CZN also provided help on specific environmental and installation management practice and were willing to participate in teleconferences with the RAND team as the material came together. We also would like to thank Ms Amy Sprunger, Director of the Desert National Wildlife Refuge, for discussing with us issues related to DNWR management.

Our colleague David Adamson provided timely and thorough editorial assistance. Gina Frost and Cassandra Tate provided administrative and final editing support. We very much appreciate the constructive comments of our three reviewers: RAND colleagues Noreen Clancy and Carolyn Wong, and Robert Brozka, Associate Director of the Center for Environmental Management of Military Lands at Colorado State University.

Finally, we thank Ray Conley, RAND-PAF Director for Manpower, Personnel and Training, for his careful reading of the document.

Abbreviations

ACC	Air Combat Command
AF	Air Force
AFB	Air Force Base
AFMC	Air Force Materiel Command
AFI	Air Force Instruction
AGL	Above Ground Level
ATC	Air Traffic Control
BLM	Bureau of Land Management
BGEPA	Bald and Golden Eagle Protection Act
CAA	Clean Air Act
CCP	Comprehensive Conservation Plan
CRP	Comprehensive Range Plan
CSAR	Combat Search and Rescue
DNWR	Desert National Wildlife Refuge/Range
DoD	Department of Defense
DOE	Department of Energy
DOI	Department of Interior
ECR	Electronic Combat Range
EIS	Environmental Impact Statement
EOD	Explosive Ordnance Disposal
ESA	Endangered Species Act
FLPMA	Federal Land Policy and Management Act
GIS	Geographic Information System
GPS	Global Positioning System
GYE	Greater Yellowstone Ecosystem
IFR	Instrument Flight Rules
MOA	Military Operating Area
MOU	Memorandum of Understanding
MRA	Minimum Requirement Analysis
MRTFB	Major Range and Test Facility Base
MSL	Mean Sea Level
NAS	National Airspace System
NEPA	National Environmental Policy Act
NNSS	Nevada National Security Site
NPS	National Park Service

NSRE	National Survey on Recreation and the Environment
NTTR	Nevada Test and Training Range
NWPS	National Wilderness Preservation System
NWR	National Wildlife Refuge
NWRS	National Wildlife Refuge System
OSD	Office of the Secretary of Defense
PSD	Prevention of Significant Deterioration
R&D	Research and Development
RMP	Range Management Plan
ROD	Record of Decision
SAF/IE	Office of the Assistant Secretary of the Air Force for Installations, Environment and Logistics
SAF/IEE	Office of the Deputy Assistant Secretary of the Air Force for Environment, Safety and Occupational Health
SECDEF	Secretary of Defense
SUA	Special Use Airspace
T&E	Test and Evaluation
T&ES	Threatened and Endangered Species
TP	Training Projectile
USAF	United States Air Force
USDA	United States Department of Agriculture
USFS	United States Forest Service
USFWS	United States Fish and Wildlife Service
UXO	Unexploded Ordnance
VFR	Visual Flight Rules
WAQ	Warrior Adventure Quest
WSA	Wilderness Study Area
WSP	Wilderness Stewardship Plan

1. Introduction

Background

The Nevada Test and Training Range (NTTR) is located in southern Nevada. As a Major Range and Test Facility Base, it is considered to be a core element of Department of Defense (DoD) Test and Evaluation (T&E) infrastructure that must be preserved as a national asset.[7] The Air Forces also considers it

> the only location in the United States where both individual and large multi-force training are provided in highly sophisticated training exercises that simulate full-scale battlefield scenarios. Such training exercises test tactics, equipment, and personnel. The advanced level of training and testing that NTTR offers is crucial to the survival of U.S. and allied military personnel and the success of the USAF mission to defend the United States and to secure and enhance U.S. interests and policies around the world.[8]

Figure 1.1 shows a general picture of the numbered/named[9] subdivisions of the NTTR and federal lands in and around the range, with an inset map that provides a sense of its size and location relative to the state of Nevada. Appendix A has a detailed description of the airspace and land that make up the NTTR, as well as the complex interactions related to the management of the land that is included in it.

---

[7] U.S. Department of Defense, *DoD Directive 3200.11, Major Range and Test Facility Base (MRTFB)*, December 27, 2007. MRTFBs are defined as "the designated core set of DoD Test and Evaluation (T&E) infrastructure and associated workforce that must be preserved as a national asset to provide T&E capabilities to support the DoD acquisition system." MRTFB "activities" are the organizations responsible for managing MRTFB capabilities and resources. The directive lists Army, Navy, Air Force, and other MRTFB activities; in addition to the NTTR, the Air Force's activities are the 30th Space Wing, Arnold Engineering Development Center, the Air Force Flight Test Center, the Utah Test and Training Range, and the 46th Test Wing, to include 46th Test Group. (Note: with the 2012 reorganization of AFMC, the 46th Test Wing was inactivated and its missions moved to the 96th Test Wing). AFI 13-212, paragraph 1.3, notes that although MRTFB activities function primarily to enable DoD test and evaluation support missions, they also may perform other missions such as operations, training, and R&D.

[8] Nellis Air Force Base, 2010, p. 8.

[9] The depiction displays the special use airspace (SUA) set aside for the NTTR by the FAA within the National Airspace System (NAS). Generally, restricted and prohibited SUA are assigned a number, which identifies them within the NAS. Military operations areas can have names. The areas in Figure 1.1 labeled Alamo A, B, and C represent restricted airspace that is not over withdrawn land. Other named restricted areas in the NTTR (such as the TPECR, or Tolicha Peak Electronic Combat Range) are primarily over withdrawn lands. (RAND discussion with Hq USAF/A30 personnel, March 19, 2014.)

Figure 1.1. Map of Federal Lands in and Around the NTTR

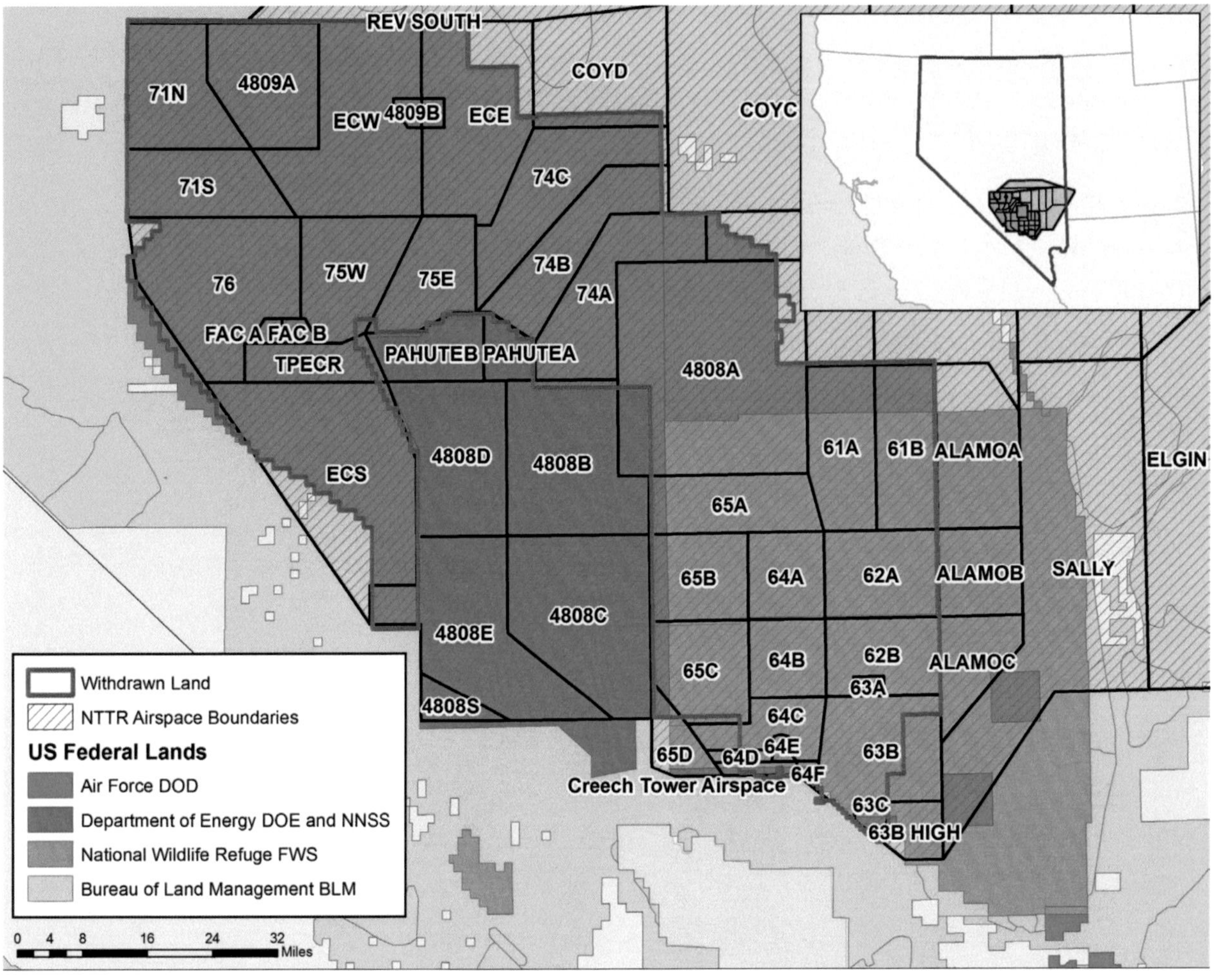

SOURCE: Map created by RAND from 1:800000. U.S. National Atlas Federal and Indian Land Areas, 2010 using ArcGIS. Version 10.1.
NOTE: The NTTR representation in the inset map includes airspace (in pink) that is not over withdrawn land.

Approximately 2.9 million acres of land in these ranges (within the orange border in the figure) have been withdrawn for use by the Air Force—that is, they have been removed from public use and reserved for military training and testing in support of national defense requirements.[10] The crosshatched areas depict NTTR airspace, which is a combination of restricted areas (primarily over withdrawn lands) and military operations areas (primarily to the

---

[10] According to the Federal Land Policy and Management Act (FLPMA), "The term 'withdrawal' means withholding an area of Federal land from settlement, sale, location, or entry, under some or all of the general land laws, for the purpose of limiting activities under those laws in order to maintain other public values in the area or reserving the area for a particular public purpose or program …" (U.S. Code of Federal Regulations, Title 43, Section 103.) The process for withdrawing lands is managed by the BLM (see U.S. Code of Federal Regulations, Title 43, Part 2300, Land Withdrawals, October 1, 2010).

east and north—see Appendix A for details). The green area is land that has been withdrawn for the Nevada National Security Site (NNSS).

The light olive-green color represents land that is part of the Desert National Wildlife Refuge (DNWR). This refuge was created by Executive Order in 1936,[11] and is now the largest wildlife refuge in the continental United States, with more than 1.6 million acres of land. The orange border of withdrawn lands shows that about half of the DNWR—approximately 842,254 acres—overlaps the NTTR.[12]

Purpose

The most recent withdrawal of the land in the NTTR from public use was authorized in October 1999 by Title XXX of Public Law 106-65, the National Defense Authorization Act for Fiscal Year 2000. This authorization expires November 6, 2021, and the Air Force is preparing to submit a request for the renewal of the withdrawal.

In preparation for this request, the Air Force asked RAND's Project Air Force to help the service understand broad strategic issues related to the future purpose and use of the withdrawn lands that make up the NTTR. One of these issues is the areas within the NTTR that are being protected as wilderness.

The part of the NTTR shown in Figure 1.1 that overlaps the DNWR is co-managed by the Air Force and the U.S. Fish and Wildlife Service (USFWS). In the early 1970's, as required by the Wilderness Act of 1964, USFWS evaluated Desert National Wildlife Refuge lands for wilderness potential and in 1974 a proposal was submitted by the secretary of the Department of the Interior (DOI) to the president and then Congress to designate a large portion of the DNWR, including a large portion of the NTTR's DNWR lands, as wilderness. Congress has not yet acted on this proposal, but until it does, the law requires that these lands must be protected and treated as wilderness. Namely, since 1974, these DNWR lands at NTTR have been managed as *de facto* wilderness. As a result, the Air Force faces restrictions on how it can use this land and the airspace above it in its training, testing, and other operations. Protecting the land as wilderness creates a situation in which some test and training restricted areas cannot be used as aircraft air-to-ground ranges. In addition, this protection limits some of the motorized vehicle travel needed for management activity (such as impact area maintenance, active wildlife management, and monitoring of radiological contamination), since motorized vehicles can only travel on existing

---

[11] President Franklin D. Roosevelt, "Establishing the Desert Game Range in Nevada," Executive Order 7373, May 20, 1936.

[12] Acreage figure for the overlap is from U.S. Department of the Air Force and U.S. Department of the Interior, "Memorandum of Understanding between the U.S. Air Force, Air Combat Command, and the Department of the Interior, U.S. Fish and Wildlife Service," draft, September 26, 2013.

roads (that are technically not part of the proposed wilderness) and cannot enter or transit wilderness areas.

The presence of these areas within the NTTR raises several important issues for Air Force management of the range as well as future withdrawal requests. Specifically, these issues involve understanding:

- The wilderness requirement of the Wilderness Act
- Changes in this requirement over the past 40 years (since these proposed wilderness areas first came under the protection of the Wilderness Act)
- Restrictions that the current status ("proposed wilderness") places on NTTR operations.

Figure 1.2 is a timeline of actions associated with the DNWR, the NTTR, and the wilderness proposal and how they fit in with the renewal of the withdrawal of land for the NTTR.

Figure 1.2. Timeline of Actions Related to the DNWR, NTTR, and Wilderness

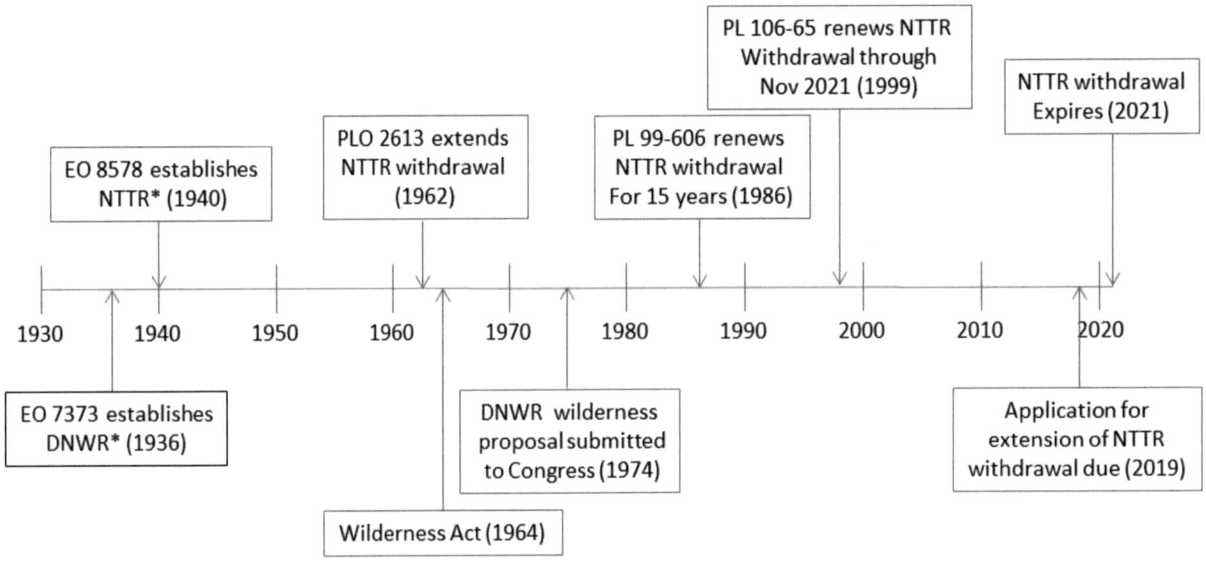

SOURCE: U.S. Department of the Air Force, *Land Use Study of the Nellis Air Force Range*, Nellis Air Force Base, Nev., September 1998, Appendix F.
NOTES: "EO" is executive order; "PL" is public law. The original name of the DNWR was the Desert Game Range. The name was changed to the Desert National Wildlife Range in 1966, but it is commonly referred to as the Desert National Wildlife Refuge. The original name of the NTTR was the Las Vegas Bombing and Gunnery Range (LVBGR). The name was changed to Nellis Air Force Range in October 1987, and was changed to the NTTR in August 2003.

The purpose of this research is to clearly describe the relationships among the NTTR, DNWR and proposed wilderness areas, discuss limitations that treating areas as wilderness imposes on Air Force operations, and propose approaches that the Air Force can take to mitigate these limitations as it prepares to renew the withdrawal of NTTR land.

Research Approach

For this research, RAND staff reviewed the relevant federal legislation, regulations, and policies that govern wilderness, withdrawn federal lands for military purposes, and National Wildlife Refuges. Key documents examined include the Wilderness Act and USFWS policies and management requirements documents for national wildlife refuges (NWRs), such as the National Wildlife Refuge Improvement Act of 1997 and Part 610, "Wilderness Stewardship," of the U.S. Fish and Wildlife Service Manual. Specific management documents for the DNWR and NTTR also were examined, such as the 2009 *DNWR Complex Final Comprehensive Conservation Plan*[13] and the 1997 *Memorandum of Understanding between the U.S. Air Force, Air Combat Command, and the Department of the Interior, U.S. Fish and Wildlife Service* that describes management of the portion of the DNWR that overlaps the NTTR. The process of assessing and proposing wilderness areas was reviewed for the DNWR, other NWRs, and some BLM lands. The literature on the value of wilderness was also briefly reviewed as part of the RAND analysis process.

RAND staff interviewed relevant NTTR staff about management goals, operations and the impact of the wilderness for NTTR operations on the NTTR portion of the DNWR. They also interviewed the manager of the DNWR about DNWR management goals and operations, as well as numerous organizations that make use of the NTTR.[14] The focus of the methodology was trying to understand the requirements that USFWS must follow in managing proposed wilderness and the DNWR, and assessing how USAF needs fit with such requirements, given the co-management role of the USAF and the USFWS on the NTTR's DNWR lands.

Outline of This Report

Chapter 2 of this report describes the proposed wilderness areas in the DNWR that overlap the NTTR, operations in those areas, and restrictions on NTTR operations that result from the proposed wilderness area status. Chapter 3 describes a range of options the Air Force has to acquire more operational flexibility on DNWR lands. Chapter 4 provides a summary and conclusions.

Many of the issues related to the NTTR and wilderness status are complex, so we have included several appendices that provide details on topics summarized in the body of this report. Appendix A describes NTTR airspace and land. Appendix B presents background material on the issue of wilderness in the United States, including the legal definitions and requirements of

---

[13] The DNWR is managed as part of the Desert National Wildlife Refuge Complex. The Complex consists of four refuges located in southern Nevada: Ash Meadows, Desert, Moapa Valley, and Pahranagat National Wildlife Refuges. For more information about the differences between the DNWR and the DNWR Complex and their management, see Appendix C.

[14] About 60 people participated in interviews.

the 1964 Wilderness Act, where the wilderness is located, and information about the value of wilderness. Appendix C provides an overview of the National Wildlife Refuge System, how National Wildlife Refuges (NWRs) are managed, an overview of the DNWR, and the details about the wilderness proposal for the DNWR. Appendix D describes the official wilderness review process that USFWS must conduct to determine if NWR lands are suitable for wilderness designation.

2. Proposed Wilderness within the DNWR and Its Impact on NTTR Operations

In this chapter, we explain the status of the DNWR proposed wilderness and the impact that this status has on NTTR operations. To set the context, we begin by providing background on U.S. wilderness laws and requirements and why and how the wilderness proposal for the DNWR was developed. Then we briefly explain the status of the proposed wilderness within the DNWR and how the DNWR is managed. Finally, we describe some NTTR operations near the proposed wilderness areas and how the proposed wilderness areas have restricted NTTR activities.

Background on U.S. Wilderness

Because of increasing "population" and "settlements" and the growth of "mechanization," Congress passed The Wilderness Act of 1964 to preserve and protect lands "in their natural condition."[15] Wilderness was defined by this Act as federal land areas that have not been significantly impacted by man and remain in a nearly natural condition. The Wilderness Act went on to specify what uses were allowed in wilderness and what activities were prohibited: "Wilderness areas shall be devoted to the public purposes of recreational, scenic, scientific, educational, conservation, and historical use."[16] Activities that are prohibited in wilderness, according to the Wilderness Act, include commercial enterprise, the building of roads and structures, and the use of mechanized vehicles, because these activities could harm or destroy the fundamental nature of the wilderness. Exceptions are made for area administration and health and safety reasons.

The Wilderness Act also created a National Wilderness Preservation System (NWPS) on federal lands to identify, preserve and protect these wilderness areas. It required the secretary of the Department of the Interior (DOI) to "review every roadless area of five thousand contiguous acres or more" of DOI lands and "report to the president his recommendation as to the suitability or non-suitability of each such area … for preservation as wilderness."[17] After the president reviews any such federal lands considered suitable for wilderness and recommends them for wilderness preservation to Congress, they become wilderness only when Congress acts to designate them as wilderness: "A recommendation of the President for designation as wilderness

[15] Public Law 88-577, Wilderness Act, September 3, 1964.

[16] Public Law 88-577, Sec. 4(b).

[17] Public Law 88-577.

shall become effective only if so provided by an Act of Congress."[18] Any lands that the president proposes as wilderness to Congress must be maintained as wilderness until Congress officially acts on the request to designate the lands as wilderness. The wilderness designation does not always preclude other use, and there may be management procedures that outline how these activities can proceed when appropriate.[19]

Status of the Proposed Wilderness within the DNWR

Given the legal requirements of the Wilderness Act, the USFWS had to review all of its national wildlife refuge (NWR) lands, including the DNWR, for their suitability for wilderness preservation; the Secretary of Interior then made wilderness proposals to the president and Congress regarding NWR lands. In the early 1970s, USFWS staff reviewed major portions of the DNWR for their suitability as wilderness, and made a "proposal to designate approximately 1.4 million acres of land within the Desert NWR as wilderness. This wilderness proposal was submitted to Congress [by the president] in 1974 but Congress has yet to act on the proposal."[20] With this original proposal, the president "recommended that Congress defer action on the proposal until a mineral survey was completed." A mineral assessment for the DNWR was "completed in 1993 as part of the mineral withdrawal, which was later completed in 1999."[21] A final environmental impact statement (EIS) for the DNWR wilderness proposal was completed in 1975. Because Congress has yet to act on this proposed wilderness area within the DNWR, "the area continues to be managed to protect its wilderness values."[22] USFWS stated in the 2009 *DNWR Complex Comprehensive Conservation Plan* (CCP), the management framework for the DNWR Complex, that it "plans to prepare a revised proposal" for the proposed wilderness areas as part of the implementation of the CCP.[23] The USFWS has yet to develop this revised proposal. It is important to note that it is not uncommon for Congress not to act on wilderness proposals for decades.[24]

---

[18] Public Law 88-577.

[19] For example, see U.S. Fish and Wildlife Service, *Desert National Wildlife Refuge Complex Ash Meadows, Desert, Moapa Valley, and Pahranagat National Wildlife Refuges: Final Comprehensive Conservation Plan and Environmental Impact Statement*, Sacramento, Calif.: U.S. Fish and Wildlife Service Pacific Southwest Region, August 2009. It contains some provision for the maintenance of Desert Sheep water "guzzlers," or containers that collect rainwater to make it available for animals. The USFWS directives require that other approved federal use is considered when setting management accommodations, as is discussed in more detail in Appendix C.

[20] U.S. Fish and Wildlife Service, 2009, Appendix I.

[21] U.S. Fish and Wildlife Service, 2009, pp. 1-28 and 1-29.

[22] U.S. Fish and Wildlife Service, 2009, p. 1-29.

[23] U.S. Fish and Wildlife Service, 2009, Appendix I.

[24] For example, USFWS has wilderness proposals located in 21 different national wildlife refuges that were submitted to Congress between 1969 and 1974 that are still awaiting congressional action. (Source: Excel

Figure 1.1 showed a map of the NTTR and how a portion of it (in what is referred to as the South Range) overlaps the DNWR. Figure 2.1 is a map of the DNWR that highlights the proposed wilderness areas within it.[25]

spreadsheet provided by the Division of Natural Resources, National Wildlife Refuge System, June, 2014.) Similarly, wilderness proposals for National Park Service and BLM lands have awaited congressional decisions for decades. A representative from the Division of Natural Resources suggested that these proposals are in a kind of limbo; many of them were probably submitted to congressional committees that no longer exist, and the only "official" location for the proposals is USFWS's realty files. Congress rarely initiates action on languishing proposals. Generally, a non-government organization like the Sierra Club will take an interest in a longstanding proposal and then encourage a congressional delegation to take it up.

[25] The NTTR is not the only military range that is associated with wildlife refuges or wilderness. For example, the Barry M. Goldwater Air Force Range in southern Arizona is bordered on the south and east by the Cabeza Prieta National Wildlife Refuge, 93 percent of which has been designated wilderness. (See University of Montana Department of Forestry and Conservation, Wilderness.net, "Wilderness.net's Cabeza Prieta Wilderness Fact Sheet," undated.) PL 106-65 states that "continued use of the Cabeza Prieta National Wildlife Refuge and Cabeza Prieta Wilderness by the Marine Corps and the Air Force to support military aviation training will remain necessary to ensure the readiness of the Armed Forces." (Public Law 106-65, National Defense Authorization Act for Fiscal Year 2000, October 5, 1999.) The Department of the Air Force, Department of the Navy, and Department of Interior have a memorandum of understanding for how this support is provided. However, unlike with the NTTR and DNWR, the refuge and wilderness areas have not been withdrawn for use by the military.

Figure 2.1. Proposed Wilderness Areas in the DNWR

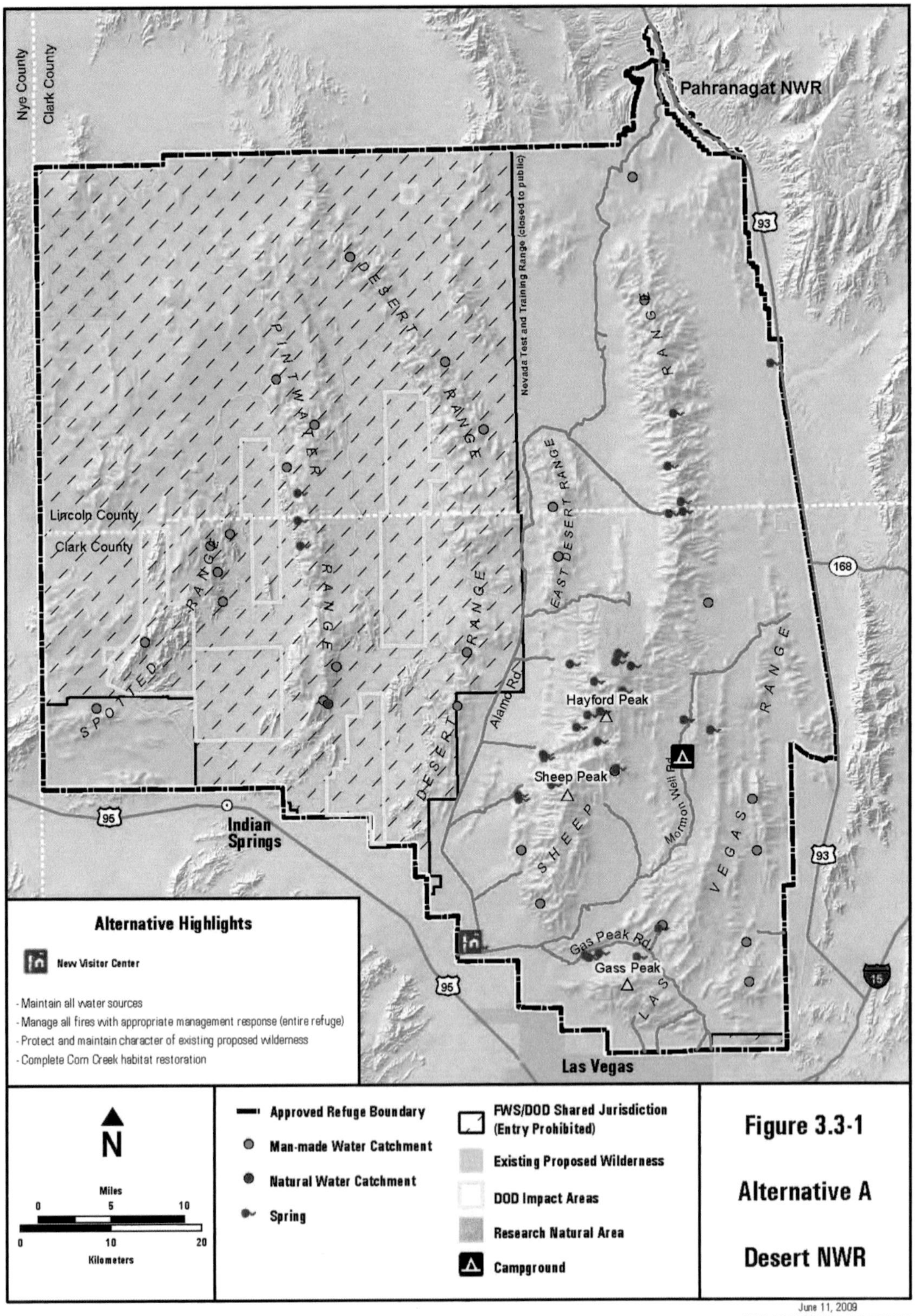

SOURCE: 2009 Final DNWR Complex Comprehensive Conservation Plan, Figure 3.3-1.

The DNWR overlap with the NTTR is shown by the hashed area in Figure 2.1, and amounts to approximately 842,254 acres. Almost 90 percent of the DNWR (about 1.4 million acres) is proposed wilderness, as shown by the tan-colored areas in Figure 2.1, and about 590,000 of those acres are in the NTTR.[26] Figure 2.1 also includes some "impact areas" in the NTTR part of the DNWR designated by yellow borders. A 1997 memorandum of understanding (MOU) between the Fish and Wildlife Service and the Air Force regarding impact areas within the NTTR part of the DNWR allows the Air Force to use about 112,000 acres in these areas for air-to-ground targeting,[27] and Public Law 106-65 transferred primary jurisdiction of these impact areas to the Air Force in 2000, with the Secretary of the Interior maintaining secondary jurisdiction for wildlife conservation purposes.[28] Transfer of jurisdiction appears to have important consequences for management of these areas.[29] The rest of the DNWR that overlaps with the NTTR is co-managed by USAF and USFWS, according to the MOU—for example, USFWS has agreed to cooperate with the Air Force in the recovery of downed aircraft and aircrew, and the Air Force has agreed to provide aircraft support for wildlife inventory and other refuge management purposes. However, other legal processes and procedures govern the management and use of a NWR and proposed wilderness areas in a NWR that affect what the Air Force and USFWS can do. These affect operational activities as well as the management and support activity of both organizations. We discuss these below.

---

[26] Acreage figures for the overlap and the proposed wilderness in the NTTR are from U.S. Department of the Air Force and U.S. Department of the Interior, 2013.

[27] U.S. Department of the Air Force and Department of the Interior, "Memorandum of Understanding between the US Air Force, Air Combat Command, and the Department of the Interior, U.S. Fish and Wildlife Service," December 1997.

[28] This is in Section 3011, paragraph (b) (3) of the Act. See U.S. Department of the Air Force and U.S. Fish and Wildlife Service, "Memorandum of Agreement for the Acquisition of Replacement Property in Nevada," July 2000. That agreement called for the Air Force to provide $15 million to USFWS to acquire lands to replace the 112,000 acres. Paragraph (b)(3) and paragraph (b)(5)(f) of Section 3011 of the 1999 Military Lands Withdrawal Act authorize such a transaction.

[29] Refuge managers are responsible for determining what activities are appropriate on the refuge and for evaluating what proposed activities are compatible with the purpose of the refuge. See U.S. Fish and Wildlife Service, *USFWS Service Manual,* Washington, D.C.: Division of Policy and Directives Management, updated August 21, 2015. Part 603 of the manual describes the process for determining appropriate uses of a refuge (603 FW 1) and the process for determining compatibility of uses. If USFWS does not have jurisdiction "over the use or the area where the use would occur, we have no authority to consider the use." (Section 603 FW 1, paragraph 1.11 A.(3)(a), added July 26, 2006). In addition, when it comes to compatibility, the manual says that compatibility provisions of the Refuge Administration Act "do not apply to activities authorized, funded, or conducted by another Federal agency that has primary jurisdiction over the area where a refuge or a portion of a refuge has been established, if those activities are conducted in accordance with a memorandum of understanding between the Secretary or the Director and the head of the Federal agency with primary jurisdiction over the area." (Section 603 FW 2, paragraph 2.10 B(5), added November 17, 2000.)

Management of the DNWR

The management structure at the DNWR includes the manager of the DNWR itself, who is located at the DNWR, and the manager of the DNWR Complex, located in Las Vegas, who oversees all four of the refuges (Ash Meadows, DNWR, Moapa Valley, and Pahranagat National Wildlife Refuge) that comprise the DNWR Complex. The manager of the DNWR Complex reports to the Regional Chief of the National Wildlife Refuge System for the USFWS Pacific Southwest Region in Sacramento, California.

According to the National Wildlife Refuge Improvement Act of 1997, USFWS must manage the DNWR based on a Comprehensive Conservation Plan (CCP) that has gone through a public review process. The 2009 DNWR Complex CCP—for which the Air Force provided some input[30]—governs the NTTR portions of the DNWR as well as the portions that are just managed by USFWS. This 2009 CCP also included an environmental impact statement (EIS) because of National Environmental Policy Act (NEPA) requirements. The CCP provides the framework for management decisions on a national wildlife refuge for 10 to 15 years and ensures "that management programs on the refuges are consistent with the mandates of the NWRS [National Wildlife Refuge System] and the purposes for which each refuge was established" and "that the management of the refuges fully considers resource priorities and management strategies identified in other federal, state, and local plans." This statement implies that USAF management needs for using the DNWR should be considered in the CCP. The CCP also must "evaluate existing and proposed uses of each refuge to ensure that they are compatible with the refuge purpose(s) as well as the maintenance of biological integrity, diversity, and environmental health."[31]

National wildlife refuges are managed for wildlife conservation and wildlife-dependent recreation. As outlined in the National Wildlife Refuge System Improvement Act of 1997, six areas of wildlife-dependent recreation are considered appropriate on refuges: hunting, fishing, wildlife observation, photography and environmental education and interpretation. A public desert bighorn sheep hunt is allowed at the DNWR, including on parts of the NTTR lands. This hunting is the only public access and use allowed on the NTTR's DNWR lands. However, all the other wildlife-dependent recreation uses occur on the rest of the DNWR.

In contrast, BLM lands are managed for multiple purposes and allow more impact on wildlife and their habitat than NWR lands. Given the mission of a NWR compared to the BLM mission, there are more restrictions on activities on a NWR than on BLM land, which means that even if the NTTR portion of the DNWR were not wilderness, USAF operations would face more restrictions on operations than on the withdrawn BLM lands portion of the NTTR. For instance,

---

[30] Appendix M of the CCP includes changes that were made in response to comments made by a representative from Nellis Air Force Base.

[31] U.S. Fish and Wildlife Service, 2009.

wildlife conservation needs are given higher priority on NWR lands than on BLM lands. Activities such as road-building on the DNWR are more restricted than on BLM lands even without any wilderness status, because a road causes potential fragmentation of the wildlife habitat and has a potential negative impact on species such as the bighorn sheep. Maintaining and restoring healthy population levels of the desert bighorn sheep within each of the six major mountain ranges of the DNWR is a major goal for the DNWR.[32] (For more information about management on NWRs and the DNWR see appendix C.) In addition, requirements of federal and state environmental laws, such as the Endangered Species Act (ESA), the National Environmental Policy Act (NEPA), and the Bald and Golden Eagle Protection Act (BGEPA) still will apply.

Given such management requirements at the DNWR, even if the proposed wilderness on the DNWR was rejected by Congress or the wilderness proposal was withdrawn, the USAF would still find it difficult to make any significant changes in its operations on the DNWR if those changes affected the lands and environment. For example, consider the USAF trying to build a road, put in a new communications site, or make another major infrastructure change on a portion of the DNWR lands that was no longer considered wilderness. First, USFWS' DNWR management likely would say the USAF could not make such a change because of its impact on the maintenance of biological integrity, diversity, and environmental health, such as the desert bighorn sheep habitat. If USFWS management said that the proposed project could be considered and assessed as an option, the USAF still would have to satisfy NEPA requirements and go through a comprehensive EIS process. In addition, since such projects are not in the current DNWR Complex CCP, the official management plan for the DNWR, the USFWS likely would need to update the CCP, and likely would require the USAF to pay for the update, since the request is for USAF needs. Updating the CCP and conducting an EIS would be an expensive and multi-year analysis process involving the assessment of multiple alternatives and extensive public input. This process could result in a recommendation not to build the new road or other infrastructure project because it impacts the DNWR mission and environmental requirements too significantly.[33]

For smaller proposed projects, that do not require NEPA or CCP changes, the USFWS still would have to give approval. USFWS staff, given NWR management requirements, could judge the impact on the maintenance of biological integrity, diversity, environmental health, or desert

---

[32] U.S. Fish and Wildlife Service, 2009, p. 1-32.

[33] At Alaska's Izembek National Wildlife Refuge, an example occurred in which a proposed road in a NWR was rejected because of ecological concerns after an almost four-year analysis process with more than 130 stakeholder meetings and an environmental impact analysis. In this proposal, the proposed road did go through some wilderness areas. However, it also involved a land exchange and Native American and other community transportation accessibility concerns. For more information see U.S. Department of the Interior, "Secretary Jewell Issues Decision on Izembek National Wildlife Refuge Land Exchange and Road Proposal," press release, December 23, 2013.

bighorn sheep populations too great and deny approval. A fundamental challenge for the Air Force is that many things it would like to do to enhance training on these lands likely are to be at least partially destructive of the desert environment and wildlife habitats, which goes against the DNWR's main mission to protect and maintain the biological integrity, diversity, and environmental health of its lands.

The proposed wilderness areas also have special management and use requirements. The USFWS Wilderness Stewardship Policy (found in Part 610 of the USFWS Field Manual) provides guidance for how to manage wilderness and proposed wilderness on NWR lands. This policy describes the process for allowing some limited prohibited activities in wilderness for management purposes. This process is called a minimum requirement analysis (MRA), which is "a decision-making process, documented in writing," that USFWS staff use to "determine if proposed refuge management activities conducted in wilderness are necessary to administer the area as wilderness" and "accomplish the purposes of the refuge." "If the activities [which could impact wilderness] are necessary, the MRA also describes how to minimize resultant impacts." USFWS conducts a MRA "for all proposed refuge management activities that involve a generally prohibited use."[34] USFWS potentially could conduct an MRA for some proposed USAF management activities on the DNWR that involve a prohibited use and then potentially allow the activities. We discuss this possibility in Chapter 3. For more information about USFWS management requirements regarding wilderness on a NWR, see appendix C.

NTTR Operations Near Proposed Wilderness Areas

Air Force operations related to Red Flag,[35] weapons instructor courses, development and operational test activity, and other flying missions currently make use of airspace above the DNWR, and the grounds within it.

Figure 2.2, which is similar to Figure 2.1 but with a different color scheme, highlights two areas where this is the case. Green shading in this figure highlights areas in the DNWR that are proposed wilderness; the hashed areas indicate withdrawn land for the NTTR.

[34] U.S. Fish and Wildlife Service, *USFWS Service Manual,* Part 610 FW 1, added November 7, 2008, pp. 3, 11, 12.

[35] "Red Flag is the Air Force's premier air-to-air combat training exercise. Participants often include both U.S. and allied nations' combat air forces. The exercise gives pilots the experience of mulitple, intensive air combat sorties in the safety of a training environment." (Nellis Air Force Base, "Exercises and Flight Operations," undated.)

Figure 2.2. Examples of DNWR Areas Affected by Air Force Training

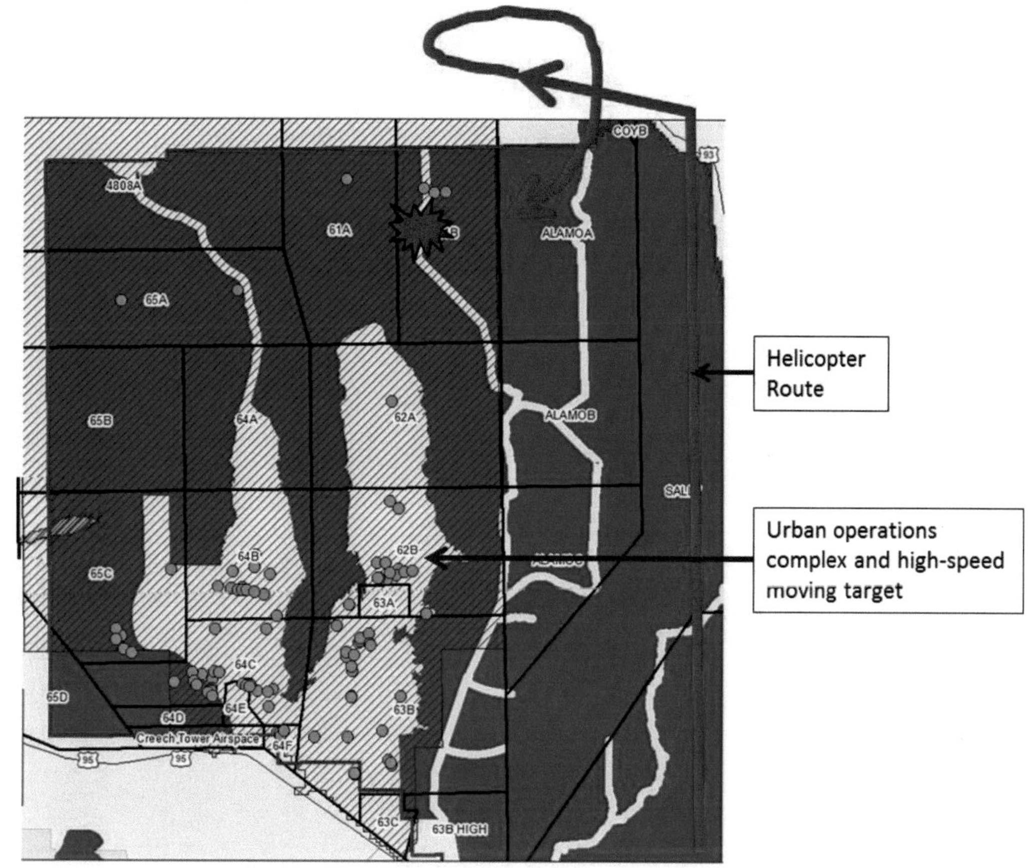

SOURCE: RAND ArcGIS files.

The red line labeled "Helicopter Route" shows a common route used during a Red Flag Combat Search and Rescue mission.[36] Helicopters fly north from Nellis Air Force Base (AFB) along the Sally Corridor (which is over DNWR-proposed wilderness land that is not part of the NTTR withdrawn land) and ultimately approach Range 61B, which is within the NTTR and is mostly proposed wilderness.[37] Ground parties participating in the exercise are present in the area marked by the red shape between Ranges 61A and 61B.[38]

---

[36] This is based on a slide from, and discussion with, ACC's 414 Combat Training Squadron at Nellis AFB.

[37] Note that at one point, a DNWR public road cuts northeast from the new Visitor Center (which is in area 63B High) through a corner of Range 63B, which is on the portion shared by Air Force-restricted lands.

[38] The Alamo areas (to the east of ranges 61 and 62) are restricted airspace areas above DNWR. Military aircraft can fly at very low altitudes at high speed and tactically maneuver over these areas. The Federal Aviation Administration establishes Restricted Areas when it is determined necessary to confine or segregate activities considered hazardous to nonparticipating aircraft. (See U.S. Department of the Air Force, *Air Force Instruction 13-201, Airspace Management*, Washington, D.C.: Secretary of the Air Force, August 21, 2012). The Air Force lands border is along the western edge of the Alamo areas.

The syllabi for the weapons instructor courses for the A-10, F-16C, and F-15E all have missions that direct the use of the south ranges, including missions that involve the urban operations complex and the high-speed moving target that are located in Range 62B. The complex and the moving target are in parts of the range that are not proposed as wilderness and for which the Air Force has primary jurisdiction.

Figure 2.2 also displays several small circles, which represent old NTTR target areas from the 1960s. Some of these, notably in Ranges 61A, 65A and 65C are located within the proposed wilderness areas of the DNWR. There is also a radioactive contamination plume from the Nevada National Security Site (NNSS) (shown as a yellow streak) which is above-ground and extends into the northern part of 65C.

Rules governing flying operations in the NTTR, including over the DNWR, are contained in the Nellis AFB addendum to Air Force Instruction 13-212.[39]

Restrictions Imposed by the Proposed Wilderness Status of the DNWR

The 2009 *NTTR Comprehensive Range Plan* (CRP) notes that approximately 882,000 acres of designated or proposed wilderness are under NTTR MOA airspace.[40] According to the CRP, laws governing wilderness areas allow for low-level overflights, flight testing and evaluation, and for the designation of special use airspace. There are, however, potential operational limitations that result from the proposed wilderness status, and the CRP points out five of them:[41]

- The placement of new communications sites[42]
- Establishing new rights of way for aircraft tracking/scoring systems
- Placement of new mobile threats or targets
- Emergency response to aircraft crashes

---

[39] U.S. Department of the Air Force, *Air Force Instruction 13-212, Volume 1, Nellis AFB Addendum A, Range Planning and Operations*, Nellis Air Force Base, Nev.: Commander 99th Air Base Wing, August 1, 2012, FOR OFFICIAL USE ONLY.

[40] Nellis Air Force Base, *Nevada Test and Training Range Comprehensive Range Plan,* Nellis Air Force Base, Nev.: 98th Range Wing, June 26, 2009, p. 60. Note that this is in addition to the proposed wilderness that is in the NTTR land overlapping the DNWR.

[41] Nellis Air Force Base, *Nevada Test and Training Range Comprehensive Range Plan,* Nellis Air Force Base, Nev.: 98th Range Wing, January 2011. This updated plan does not list these potential limitations, but includes the DNWR as an environmental issue that could pose limitations to NTTR operations (see page 91 of the document).

[42] There are examples of accommodations being made for new construction. For example, PL 106-65 allows for the possibility of new equipment being placed in the Cabeza Wilderness in Arizona (near the Goldwater Range): "The upgrade or replacement of existing associated ground instrumentation or the installation of new associated ground instrumentation shall not be precluded by the existing designation of lands within the Cabeza Prieta National Wildlife Refuge as wilderness to the extent that the Secretary of the Interior, after consultation with the Secretary of the Navy and the Secretary of the Air Force, determines that such actions, considered both individually and cumulatively, create similar or less impact than the existing ground instrumentation permitted by the Arizona Desert Wilderness Act of 1990." (Public Law 106-65, 1999).

- Recovery activities related to dropped objects or aircraft crashes

The 2009 CRP indicated that none of these limitations had any mission impact related to MOA usage, but the 2011 CRP did not make the same explicit statement. However, restrictions in the areas of proposed wilderness in the DNWR that overlap the South Range of the NTTR have the potential to affect range operations in three broad categories: testing and training, range management, and environmental management.

Testing and Training

The 1997 MOU places the following limits on testing and training activities:

- Ground operations are limited to existing training and testing facilities that are below 4,000 feet mean sea level (MSL)
- Aircrew flying over the ranges overlapping the DNWR will remain above 2,000 feet above ground level (AGL) unless a lower altitude is required for tactical training.[43]
- The placement or relocation of threats or targets is restricted to existing sites. "The construction or relocation of any road, trail, target, target area, or any military facility on the refuge will not commence without proper environmental analyses and consultation with the [U.S. Fish and Wildlife] Service"[44] – which effectively means that targets cannot be placed above 4,000 feet MSL
- The land space available to change target scenarios is limited.

Concern about potential limitations on the placement or relocation of threats and targets and the availability of land to change target scenarios is understandable, as the Air Force desires flexibility to develop training in response to future threats, but some of these limitations have affected the ability to train for recent operations. For example, we were told in interviews that it would be useful to be able to place targets high on mountainsides in the range (above 4,000 feet MSL) in order to simulate situations that were encountered by pilots responding to threats in Afghanistan.

Range Management

Air Force Instruction (AFI) 13-212 requires periodic clearance of targets on the range, to include "the removal or disposal of all ordnance, inert ordnance debris, Training Projectile (TP) ammunition, and other range debris reasonably possible to detect (normally down to four inches in size)."[45]

---

[43] This restriction is also in U.S. Department of the Air Force, 2012, Nellis Supplement, paragraph 2.2.3.

[44] U.S. Department of the Air Force and Department of the Interior, 1997.

[45] U.S. Department of the Air Force, 2012, paragraph 7.3. Schedules for cleanup vary, with different types being accomplished on six-month, yearly, and biennial schedules.

According to those responsible for cleanup operations at the NTTR, wilderness restrictions (especially related to the construction of access roads and the use of vehicles for cleanup) cost cleanup crews an enormous amount of time. This is a particular problem for Range 61, which, as we saw above, is used by helicopters for combat search and rescue (CSAR) practice and is located in the north-central portion of the southern range. Instead of being able to drive directly north from Nellis AFB to Range 61, crews must drive a circuitous route that takes them east to the border of the DNWR that is outside the NTTR, then north along the eastern border of the DNWR until they can head west to a northern access road to the range. This drive involves explosive ordnance disposal (EOD) equipment, tanks, and "snippers" (large machinery used to cut up damaged targets). Without wilderness restrictions, it might be possible to construct a road through the mountains that would allow easier access, and this could save as much as five hours of travel time.[46]

Environmental Management

A Nellis AFB biologist told us that the proposed wilderness status restricts some access by motorized vehicles, which affects the ability to conduct timely wildlife monitoring and surveys of key plant, animal, and other species. USFWS biologists face the same type of restrictions in their wildlife monitoring activities. In addition, official USFWS procedures in place, such as the MRA process, allow some limited prohibited uses, such as limited motorized vehicle use, to help with wildlife surveys and other NWR management needs. In fact, the Nellis AFB biologist noted that Nellis personnel are allowed to use helicopters to survey golden eagle nesting areas in the proposed wilderness areas.

Even if the proposed wilderness status were eliminated, as discussed earlier, the NWR requirements and other national and state environmental laws still would apply, such as the ESA, NEPA and BGEPA. Bighorn sheep populations also have special status, not just because of DNWR goals, but also because they are protected by the state of Nevada. In particular, USFWS DNWR and state wildlife managers are concerned about activities that might affect the winter lambing period. Interestingly, the overflights conducted as part of the eagle nesting surveys is one of these activities. While the Air Force has not been given any written restrictions on overflights of sheep areas, it currently voluntarily avoids low flights over sheep during lambing.

Wilderness Can Be a Useful Tool for the Air Force

Wilderness is not always bad for the Air Force. In fact, in some cases, wilderness areas on other federal lands actually can benefit Air Force testing, training, and other installation and range operations. Wilderness areas can help prevent encroachment and incompatible

---

[46] Comments related to Range 61 are from interviews conducted at the NTTR on October 29, 2013.

development near installations and test and training ranges. Wilderness is a tool that could benefit NTTR operations by helping to prevent encroachment on nearby BLM, FWS, and other federal lands.

First, wilderness status protects an area from human structures being built on it, such as wind farms, solar towers, private homes, and resort developments. All of them are key encroachment concerns for the NTTR. The first two activities cause operational concerns and the latter two generate human noise complaints.[47] Because of the growth of Las Vegas during the last 20 to 30 years, there has been pressure in Nevada to develop more large-scale energy projects on federal lands and to open up more of these areas for suburban development activities. BLM and even some USFWS lands near NTTR operations are at risk for such developments. Some BLM lands along Highway 93 under the NTTR MOA have been sold off or exchanged for local development interests. One private development effort directly east of Highway 93 and the DNWR which could become a significant encroachment concern for the NTTR (because it is under the MOA in the Sally Corridor) is the Coyote Springs development effort. The Coyote Springs development is a plan to build more than 150,000 homes on 40,000 acres, along with almost 12 golf courses, businesses, schools, parks and other facilities. This development has not been completed because of the economic downturn; however, a golf course is operational and major investments in water and electrical infrastructure have been made, so it could still be developed in the future.[48] A major power line recently was completed down the eastern DNWR border, running from western Wyoming to Las Vegas to help stabilize the western power grid. Another one is in the planning stages.[49] Similarly, proposals have been made for wind farms and solar towers on BLM lands to the east and northeast of the NTTR. Congress even has taken away some parcels of DNWR lands near Highway 93 because of such development interests. Such BLM and USFWS federal lands always are at the risk of being developed, but wilderness areas are less likely to face development pressures given their special protection as wilderness.[50] Growth in the Las Vegas area has been slowed because of the slow economy, but will likely

---

[47] For more information about such encroachment concerns, see Beth E. Lachman, Anny Wong, and Susan A. Resetar, *The Thin Green Line: An Assessment of DoD's Readiness and Environmental Protection Initiative to Buffer Installation Encroachment,* Santa Monica, Calif.: RAND Corporation, MG-612-OSD, 2007.

[48] For information about this proposed development see Jennifer Robison, "Dream of Coyote Springs development still years away from reality," *Las Vegas Review-Journal*, October 26, 2013.

[49] RAND discussions with DNWR and NTTR personnel, April 2014.

[50] Congress could technically remove wilderness status from a piece of federal property, but this is unlikely to happen given federal policies and interests regarding wilderness. Selling off or allowing the development of a piece of non-wilderness federal property is much more common, especially near Las Vegas. DNWR land that is protected as wilderness can act as a buffer by limiting public access to that of foot or horse traffic. A current public access area where this works is under the Alamo areas and east of the Air Force-withdrawn lands border. The director of the DNWR reported that her personnel have turned away people on off-road vehicles in these areas. (Discussions with DNWR, April 2014.)

increase again in the future and create more encroachment concerns for the NTTR, as other military installations have experienced.[51]

Second, wilderness areas help protect biodiversity. Loss of biodiversity can be a significant encroachment concern because as biodiversity declines, more species tend to become threatened and endangered species (T&ESs) or other species of concern. This means that their habitat needs special protection, which can restrict military testing and training operations.[52] Consider the golden eagle, which is currently not a T&ES, but is protected by the Bald and Golden Eagle Protection Act and is a species of concern in Nevada. The golden eagle nests on the NTTR and nearby BLM lands. It also can face some threats from wind-farm developments. If this species were to decline significantly to become a T&ES, it could cause restrictions on NTTR operations. Wilderness areas on BLM and non-NTTR DNWR lands can help protect the species' habitat and help prevent it from becoming a T&ES.

Some military staff have been concerned that wilderness areas can lead to noise complaints because of aircraft overflights, but such complaints are not nearly as significant as residential development complaints, especially because wilderness areas do not attract that many visitors. In addition, it is acknowledged in wilderness guidance that aircraft noise can occur anywhere and that this does not preclude an area from becoming wilderness or necessarily negate all wilderness experiences.[53]

Thus, ironically, wilderness on BLM lands and proposed wilderness areas on the DNWR non-NTTR lands actually benefits the NTTR by helping to prevent encroachment, even though it restricts the NTTR on those DNWR lands. Given this situation, the Air Force should try to take advantage of wilderness as a tool in places where it can help the NTTR and other Air Force operations.

---

[51] For more information about the impact and pressures of past and future encroachment concerns on military installations see Beth E. Lachman, Agnes Gereben Schaefer, Nidhi Kalra, Scott Hassell, Kim Curry Hall, Aimee E. Curtright, and David E. Mosher, *Key Trends That Will Shape Army Installations of Tomorrow*, Santa Monica, Calif.: RAND Corporation, MG-1255-A, 2013; and Lachman, Wong, and Resetar, 2007.

[52] Lachman, Wong, and Resetar, 2007.

[53] See U.S. Fish and Wildlife Service, *USFWS Service Manual,* Part 610 FW 2, added November 7, 2008, paragraph 2.8. "The Wilderness Act and the Administration Act do not prohibit the use of aircraft over a wilderness area. The Federal Aviation Administration (FAA) is responsible for managing commercial and private air space. The FAA has established 2,000 feet (600 meters) above ground level as the minimum altitude advisory for refuges, including designated wilderness areas (see FAA Advisory Circular 91-36c)."

3. Air Force Options to Acquire More Operational Flexibility on DNWR Lands

Given our analysis of the legal, policy and management requirements regarding wilderness and the DNWR, the USAF has a range of approaches it could take to acquire more operational flexibility on the NTTR's DNWR lands. All of these options involve working with USFWS and within official USFWS processes to meet USAF objectives. These open and transparent processes help decision-makers and interested parties balance national security needs and the benefits of wilderness. In looking at this list of options, it is important to consider the personnel levels at which each agency should be working with the other.

We have grouped these options into six main areas and describe each below, along with some pros and cons.

First, the USAF could try to get USFWS to withdraw the wilderness proposal for the DNWR lands that fall within the NTTR. The strongest argument would be that the Air Force needs the wilderness restrictions removed for its testing and training mission. Another argument could be that these lands may no longer even meet the wilderness requirement, because conditions have changed so much over the last 40 years. On the surface, this seems like the easiest and most straightforward option for the USAF to acquire more operational flexibility, but it is more complex than it seems. According to USFWS Wilderness Stewardship Policy (610 FW), USFWS officially can withdraw a wilderness proposal for a NWR if it has determined the lands are no longer suitable for wilderness designation.

However, the problem with such a withdrawal request is that it likely involves withdrawing all the proposed wilderness lands, including the parts of the DNWR that are outside the NTTR lands. Partially or totally withdrawing the DNWR wilderness proposal might cause political problems for the USFWS and DNWR: Public and environmental groups might consider filing a lawsuit over the issue targeting the USFWS and the USAF. In any case, USFWS is not likely to support withdrawing the entire proposal or even part of it. In addition, the USFWS may be required to do an analysis to justify withdrawing all or part of the proposal. Since this option involves the Congress and the president, it has much more significant political implications than some of the other options, which would involve activity more localized at the "worker" level within the USFWS and the USAF. This option would require headquarters-level USAF staff discussing the option with headquarters-level DOI staff. Even with these potential downsides, it still may be worth senior USAF officials diplomatically asking senior officials at DOI if such a possibility is feasible and what the political implications might be. However, before making the request, the USAF should consider the political implications and the potential impact on relationships with DOI and USFWS.

A second, more feasible, option is for the USAF to work with the USFWS to have the USFWS include more of the USAF operational considerations in the DNWR Complex CCP implementation of the "revised proposal" for the DNWR proposed wilderness areas. The DNWR Complex CCP of 2009 recognized that things have changed during the last few decades and stated that it was going to submit a revised proposal regarding the DNWR proposed wilderness area as part of the CCP implementation

> which includes technical corrections to the existing proposed wilderness such as: correcting overlap with US Air Force's bombing range; allowing repair/relocation of hazardous sections of roads; and allowing the use of helicopters to repair/maintain water developments and access remote areas for wildlife surveys. Details of these revisions will be provided in a revised proposal.[54]

This revised proposal during the CCP implementation process is an opportunity for the USAF to try to acquire some operational changes in the NTTR's DNWR areas to meet some of the USAF management and mission needs. As stated earlier, the CCP process is supposed to be considering other federal agencies' management needs in their role at the Refuge, so the USAF could negotiate for some operational activity changes regarding the proposed wilderness areas. The USAF should develop some specific proposals to present to the USFWS, and perhaps start by suggesting one idea that would have the least impact on the proposed wilderness areas. Having specific details about why it is important to the mission and would not significantly impact wildlife and habitat would be an important part of the argument. This option involves NTTR staff working directly with DNWR's USFWS staff. When making such a proposal, the USAF should consider USFWS management needs. It should perhaps best begin by asking DNWR management about its needs and wants in the process of co-managing the NTTR part of the DNWR. USAF staff are much more likely to be successful in obtaining what they want for NTTR operations on the DNWR by offering the DNWR management staff something that they need or want for their DNWR mission. This option may need to be considered at the intermediate level, or at the Washington D.C., Headquarters level, if contentious issues arise at the local level.

A third option is for the USAF to work with USFWS to revise the 1997 USAF-USFWS MOU regarding the DNWR. According to the DNWR CCP, a revised MOU was supposed to be completed by 2012. This MOU process is a good opportunity for the USAF to negotiate with USFWS to acquire more operational flexibility within the NTTR DNWR lands. USFWS staff wrote a revised draft MOU in 2011 and sent it to the USAF, who returned it to the DNWR staff in 2013. According to the manager of the DNWR, this draft MOU is currently with DNWR's "realty division" for review. As of July 2015 this MOU was still under negotiation. Unfortunately, this draft MOU did not include any special considerations for easing some of the

---

[54] U.S. Fish and Wildlife Service, 2009, Appendix I.

restrictions in the proposed wilderness areas of the NTTR's DNWR lands. However, since the MOU is not finalized, the USAF could approach USFWS and suggest such an idea, then negotiate with USFWS about revising the MOU. This is an ongoing process with NTTR, Nellis AFB and ACC staff working with USFWS staff at the DNWR. If contentious issues arise, this option may need to be raised to the AF headquarters level to move the effort forward. In fact, given the MOU's current status, headquarters-level Air Force staff would be the appropriate level to make such a request. Unfortunately, NEPA as well as NWR rules may apply, including requiring a MRA for refuge management activities, which could make easing some restrictions in the MOU infeasible without a lengthy delay in the process.

In a fourth option, the USAF could work with the USFWS to have USFWS conduct an MRA for DNWR management activities, including USAF management considerations such as allowing the building of a new dirt road. Such a road could be useful for both USAF mission purposes and for DNWR wildlife management needs. As discussed earlier, the USFWS uses the MRA process to allow prohibited-use activities in wilderness areas within an NWR for management purposes. The USAF could state how this process is supposed to consider all management needs for the DNWR, including USAF needs for testing and training operations. As the 2009 DNWR Complex CCP states, "The management of refuges fully consider … management strategies in other federal, state, and local plans."[55] As stated earlier, an MRA is conducted when an activity involves a prohibited use, but is needed to "accomplish the purpose of the refuge." USFWS staff potentially could conduct an MRA for some proposed USAF management activities on the DNWR that involve a prohibited use and then be used to allow those activities. This option involves USAF's NTTR staff working with USFWS' DNWR management. However, if local USFWS staff at the DNWR do not consider an official NTTR staff request for an MRA, this request may also have to be initiated at the level of the Office of the Assistant Secretary of the Air Force for Installations, Environment and Logistics or higher.

A fifth option would involve the USAF trying to get the USFWS to conduct a wilderness review process to see if NTTR's DNWR lands still are suitable for the wilderness designation. "A wilderness review is the process we [USFWS staff] follow to identify and recommend for congressional designation Refuge System lands and waters that merit inclusion in the National Wilderness Preservation System (NWPS),"[56] "This process includes interagency and tribal coordination, public involvement, and National Environmental Policy Act (NEPA) compliance." This means that an environmental impact statement is required. Wilderness reviews usually are conducted as part of a scheduled CCP or CCP revision, and are time-consuming and expensive. At a minimum, USFWS conducts wilderness reviews every 15 years through the CCP process.

---

[55] U.S. Fish and Wildlife Service, 2009, p. 1-2.

[56] U.S. Fish and Wildlife Service, *USFWS Service Manual,* Part 610 FW 4, added November 7, 2008, paragraph 4.4a.

USFWS "may conduct a wilderness review as part of a CCP revision any time that significant new information becomes available, ecological conditions change, major refuge expansion occurs, or when we [USFWS staff] identify the need to do so during plan review."[57] NTTR's USAF staff could ask USFWS' DNWR management about the wilderness review process and if it is reasonable to conduct one, given the changes during the last 40 years. However, USFWS management is not likely to be willing to do an official wilderness review, given the time and expense of this process, and because it did not conduct one during the 2009 CCP update, which would have been the logical time for such a review. (For more information about the wilderness review process, see Appendix D.)

In addition, given our review of the wilderness requirements, how the USFWS conducts wilderness reviews, and the environmental stewardship requirements and procedures of the USAF on the NTTR, it is possible that much of the proposed wilderness on the NTTR part of the DNWR still would meet wilderness requirements. However, if the USAF took a more active role in such a process, it might be possible to get parts of the now-proposed wilderness property excluded from the proposal. It is not uncommon for small parcels to be added in or taken out of a proposed wilderness area over time. For example, it is possible that the USAF could get the radioactive plume area and some of the old target sites in the proposed wilderness areas removed from the proposed wilderness status. Even though this option is challenging and may not totally remove the proposed wilderness areas on the NTTR, it may be worth pursuing because it could potentially help provide more operational flexibility on the NTTR's DNWR lands.

Finally, as noted in Chapter 2, Public Law 106-65 transferred primary jurisdiction of several impact sites within the NTTR/DNWR overlap area to the Air Force, with the secretary of the Interior maintaining secondary jurisdiction for wildlife conservation purposes. The transfer of primary jurisdiction for the impact areas to the Air Force seems to imply a great deal of flexibility for the Air Force in what it does in those areas, since 603 FW1 and 603 FW2 state that USFWS has no authority to consider the appropriateness of a use if it does not have jurisdiction, and compatibility provisions for use do not apply in certain circumstances if another agency has primary jurisdiction. It may be possible for the Air Force to explore with USFWS the possibility of transferring primary jurisdiction to the Air Force of other areas that are considered crucial to the maintenance of testing and training capabilities. Note, however, that the transfer of jurisdiction for the impact areas involved lands that were not proposed wilderness; further research is necessary to determine the possibility of using this approach for areas that are proposed wilderness. For instance, if USFWS agreed to conduct the wilderness review described in option 5, the Air Force could propose changes in primary jurisdiction for areas that no longer meet wilderness criteria.

---

57 *USFWS Service Manual,* Part 610 FW 4, p. 44.

DNWR access to the NTTR already is restricted, and the Air Force could claim that it accomplishes its refuge management goals through its environmental and natural-resource management activities and compliance with the 1960 Sikes Act.[58] With a transfer of primary jurisdiction and a carefully negotiated memorandum of understanding, it might be possible for the Air Force and the USFWS to satisfy, in large part, their sometimes conflicting goals. A potential downside of this option is cost: The transfer of primary jurisdiction of the impact areas required that the Air Force provide USFWS with $15 million for the acquisition of replacement lands.[59]

It is important to note that these options are not mutually exclusive, and synergies could result from pursuing more than one of them simultaneously, such as the second and fourth options. Also, not all of the options require the same amounts of time or resources. Many of these options incur costs for both the Air Force and the USFWS, but the latter's costs are likely to be higher because of the management procedures and requirements that the agency must follow regarding an NWR. For instance, the fifth option is the most costly (with most of the cost burden falling on USFWS) and the most time-consuming. Since option five requires conducting a NEPA process, including developing an EIS and having extensive public involvement, this process would take several years. It is unclear how costly and time-consuming some of the other options would be; the cost and time partly depend on DNWR and USFWS implementation procedures and requirements regarding some of these proposed processes. The second option seems the most practical and least costly. It is also the most diplomatic and would keep decision-making at the local working level.

The USAF has a difficult diplomatic challenge in working with USFWS and should clearly articulate its needs, yet also be understanding about USFWS management's perspectives and requirements since the USAF and USFWS co-manage the NTTR part of the DNWR. Looking for synergies and mutual benefits in co-management is a good strategic approach. However, the USAF may need to have more-senior levels of its management take the lead in negotiations with USFWS, especially when policy and higher-level USAF priorities are involved. The USAF also may want to pursue one of the more challenging options, such as the fifth option, but the USAF needs to consider the full range of political implications of such actions, especially on the long-term local working relationship between the NTTR and the USFWS.

---

58 The Sikes Act requires the DoD to "carry out a program to provide for conservation and rehabilitation of natural resources on military installations." It also directs the development of an integrated natural resource management plan (INRMP) for each military installation. The overall philosophy behind the Nellis AFB INRMP is "to provide natural resource management guidance within the context of the ecosystems management concept," and the "primary principles of the USAF for ecosystem management will be to maintain or restore ecological processes, hydrologic processes, and native ecosystem types across their natural range where practical and consistent with the military mission." (see Nellis Air Force Base, 2010, p. 18).

59 U.S. Department of the Air Force and U.S. Fish and Wildlife Service, 2000. It called for the Air Force to provide $15 million to USFWS to acquire lands to replace the 112,000 acres.

4. Conclusion

The renewal of the land withdrawal for the NTTR involves several players, including the Air Force, BLM, USFWS, DOI, DOE and the State of Nevada. As part of its withdrawal request, the Air Force must fully document its purpose and needs for the withdrawn land; this will be the subject of a follow-on RAND document. This paper has focused on the wilderness issue related to the DNWR because of the restrictions it places on NTTR operations. Although the proposed wilderness on NTTR's DWNR lands technically is separate from the withdrawal issue, dealing with the issue now may provide the Air Force an opportunity to gain flexibility in its operations in the South Range, which is important for future operations and missions of the NTTR.[60] The two primary players with respect to the wilderness issue are the Air Force and the USFWS.

Because of use restrictions there are desired range activities that cannot be conducted on some lands in the South Range. The lack of access to areas above 3,200 feet, where impact areas or targets and other ground training infrastructure can be located, is a serious limitation.[61] At least three of these areas have no current target complexes. The Air Force could accept the operational restrictions imposed from the proposed wilderness and proceed with the land-withdrawal renewal with the present restrictions in place. There is some concern, however, that this requires modifications to test and training missions conducted in the South Range that reduce training realism. In addition, significant costs are a consequence of the proposed wilderness protection. These costs are related to range maintenance and to the cost associated with flying further (e.g., to the North Range) to accomplish missions, which otherwise would be accommodated on the closer South Range areas. Accepting the current restrictions without potential mitigation measures keeps costs at today's levels.

The USAF has a range of options to pursue for acquiring more operational flexibility on NTTR's DNWR proposed wilderness lands that are outside the withdrawal process. By specifically identifying what operational activities they would want and where they should be conducted, NTTR staff should work with USFWS to pursue options using the official legal and policy procedures that USFWS follows regarding the management of proposed wilderness areas in NWRs.

---

[60] The affected restricted areas are the ones closest to Nellis AFB and thereby when used require fewer non-productive en route flying hours to reach and return to base. There are also cost implications for NTTR maintenance and lands stewardship responsibilities.

[61] In discussions with NTTR personnel on October 29, 2013, we were told that, effectively, areas above 3,200 feet MSL were considered to be wilderness.

By pursuing such options in collaboration with USFWS, the Air Force has the opportunity to benefit the mission. Some of these options should be coordinated at the local level; some require Air Force Headquarters involvement. NTTR needs to develop strategies appropriately.

Appendix A. General Description of the NTTR

The NTTR, located in southern Nevada, includes both airspace and land. The NTTR airspace comprises roughly 12,000 square nautical miles, and extends about 150 miles west to east and 110 miles north to south.[62] Figure A.1 shows that while it is mostly contained in Nevada north of Las Vegas, a portion of the airspace extends into Utah.

Figure A.1. Location of NTTR Airspace in Nevada and Utah

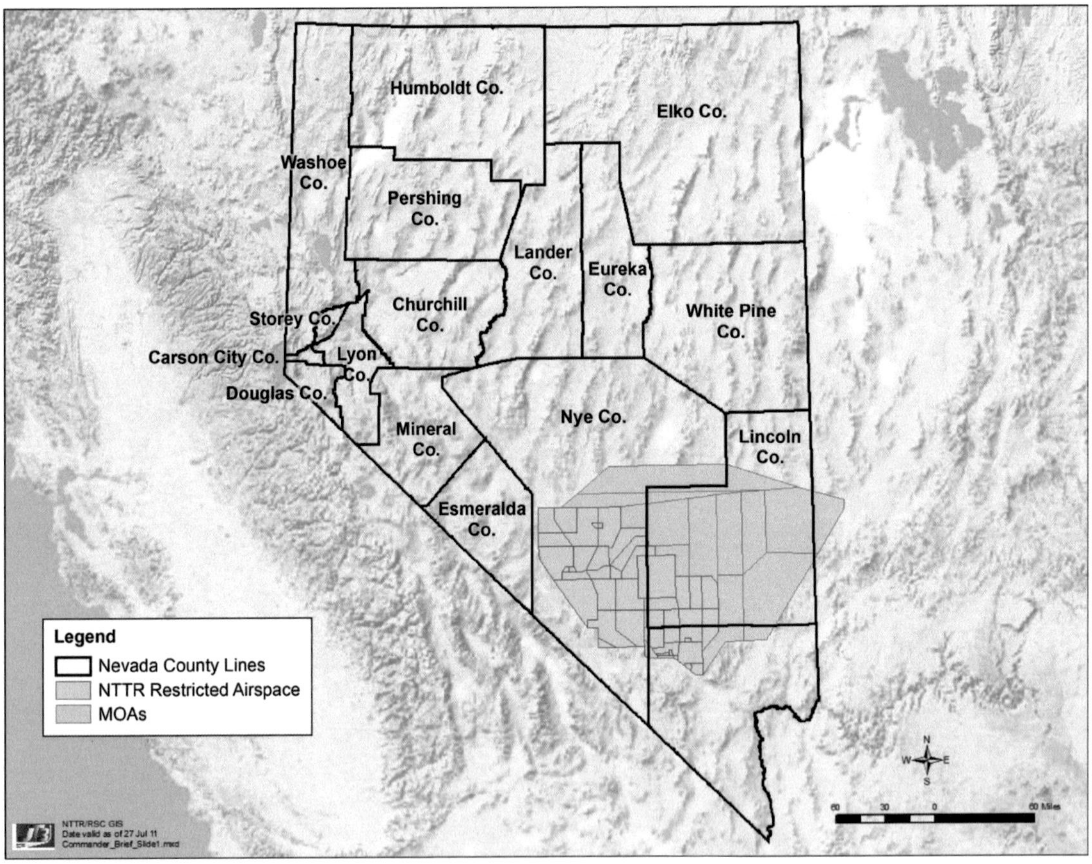

SOURCE: PowerPoint briefing "XPN Brief for CC," February 2013.

NTTR Airspace

The airspace in the NTTR includes both MOAs and Restricted Areas. MOAs are established for the purpose of separating certain military training activities from other air traffic. When an

[62] Airspace and land area figures are from Nellis Air Force Base, 2011, p. 46.

MOA is being used, aircraft operating under instrument flight rules (IFR) that are not participating in the military activity may be cleared to fly through it if air traffic control (ATC) can provide appropriate separation. Otherwise, ATC will reroute or restrict nonparticipating IFR traffic.[63] Commercial or private pilots operating under visual flight rules (VFR) are allowed to fly through active MOAs, but are advised to contact the controlling agency for military aircraft traffic advisories. MOAs are designated to "contain nonhazardous military flight activities including, but not limited to, air combat maneuvers, air intercepts, [and] low altitude mission tactics."[64]

Restricted areas contain airspace identified by an area on the surface of the earth within which the flight of aircraft, while not wholly prohibited, is subject to restrictions.[65] Restricted Areas are established when determined necessary to confine or segregate activities considered hazardous to nonparticipating aircraft.[66]

Figure A.2 shows the division of NTTR airspace into two MOAs (Reveille to the north and the Desert MOA in the east) and four Restricted Areas: R-4806, R-4807, R-4808, and R-4809.[67]

---

[63] See U.S. Federal Aviation Administration, *Aeronautical Information Manual,* Section 4, "Special Use Airspace," April 3, 2014.

[64] U.S. Department of the Air Force, 2012, p.48.

[65] U.S. Federal Aviation Administration, 2014.

[66] U.S. Department of the Air Force, p. 49.

[67] "The NTTR is ... defined as the external boundaries of the Desert and Reveille Military Operations Area (MOA)/Air Traffic Control Assigned Airspace (ATCAA), restricted areas R-4806 East and West, R-4807 Alpha and Bravo, R-4808 North and South, and R-4809." (Nellis Air Force Base, 2009, p. 20).

Figure A.2. MOAs and Restricted Areas in the NTTR

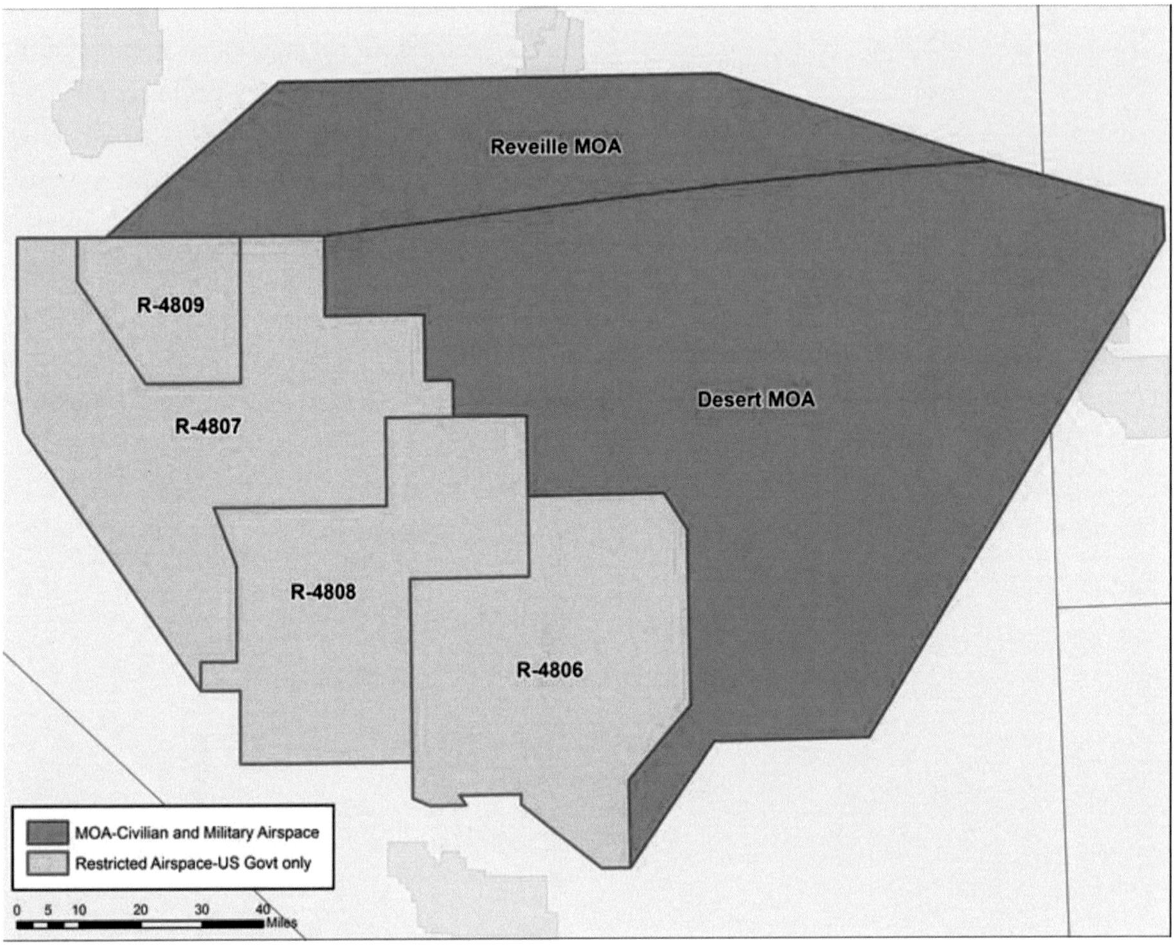

SOURCE: Map created by RAND from 1:800000. U.S. National Atlas Federal and Indian Land Areas, 2010 using ArcGIS. Version 10.1. and ArcGIS data from NTTR.

According to the *2011 Comprehensive Range Plan*, the two MOAs are used primarily for air-to-air combat training. They also are useful during large-force exercises because attacking aircraft can maneuver in them prior to entry into the restricted areas. R-4806 is used for testing, training, and weapons school training; R-4807 is an electronic combat range (ECR) that also is used for munitions training; R-4808 is used primarily by the Nevada National Security Site (NNSS),[68] and R-4809 is an electronic combat range.

The NTTR MOAs and Restricted Areas are subdivided into numbered and named areas as shown in Figure A.3; these subdivisions allow the development of areas with different range classifications and capabilities.

[68] The NNSS will be discussed further in the section about the land portion of the NTTR.

Figure A.3. Subdivisions of NTTR Airspace

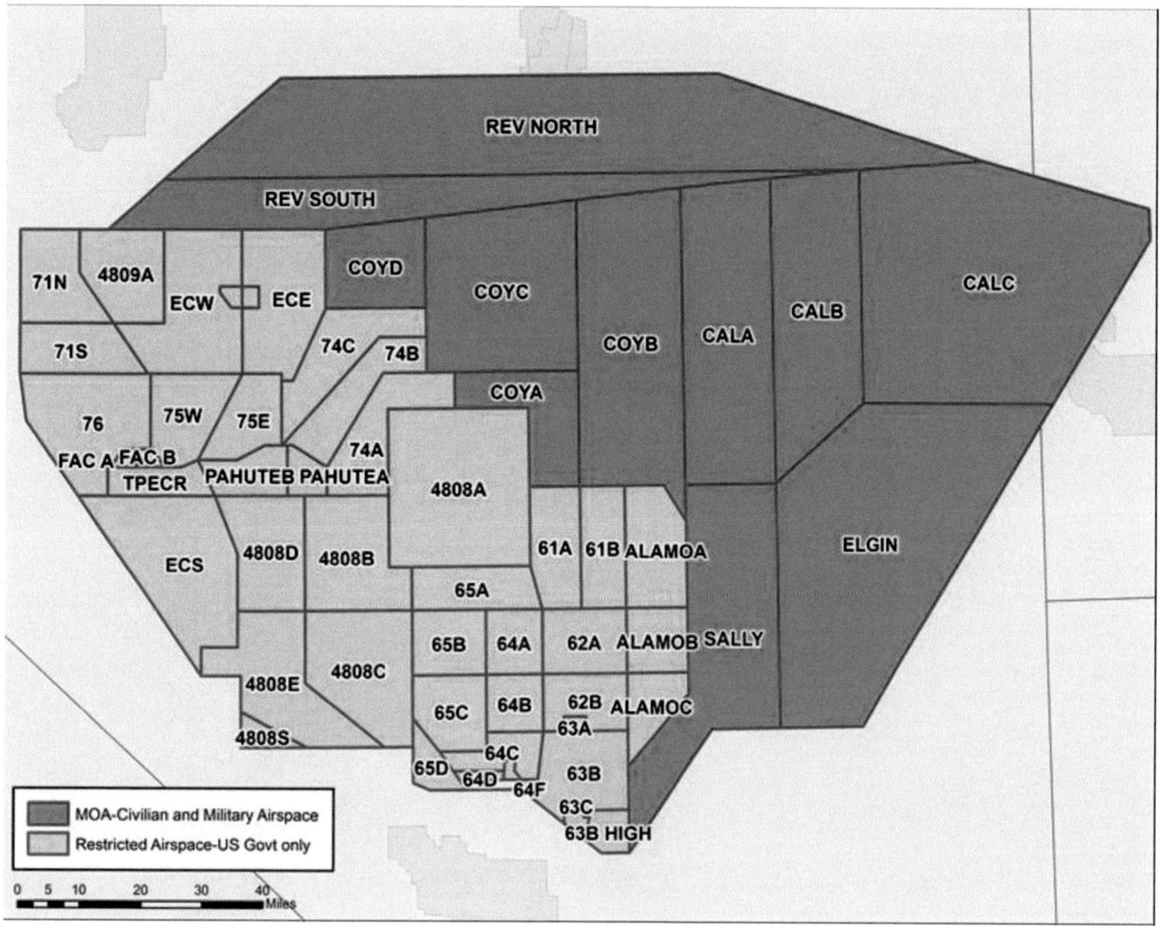

SOURCE: Map created by RAND from 1:800000. U.S. National Atlas Federal and Indian Land Areas, 2010 using ArcGIS. Version 10.1. and ArcGIS data from NTTR.

NTTR Land

The NTTR includes 2,919,890 acres of Department of Interior lands that have been withdrawn from public use. This action was accomplished by The Military Lands Withdrawal Act of 1999.[69] Figure A.4 shows the extent of this withdrawn land and how its boundaries compare with those of the airspace above it.

---

[69] This is part of Public Law 106–65. The Military Land Withdrawal is in Title XXX of the law. The land description is in Section 3011, paragraph (b) (4): "The public lands and interests in lands withdrawn and reserved ... comprise approximately 2,919,890 acres of land in Clark, Lincoln, and Nye Counties, Nevada, as generally depicted on the map entitled 'Nevada Test and Training Range, Proposed Withdrawal Extension,' dated April 22, 1999 and filed in accordance with Section 3012."

Figure A.4. Comparison of Withdrawn Land Boundaries and Airspace Boundaries

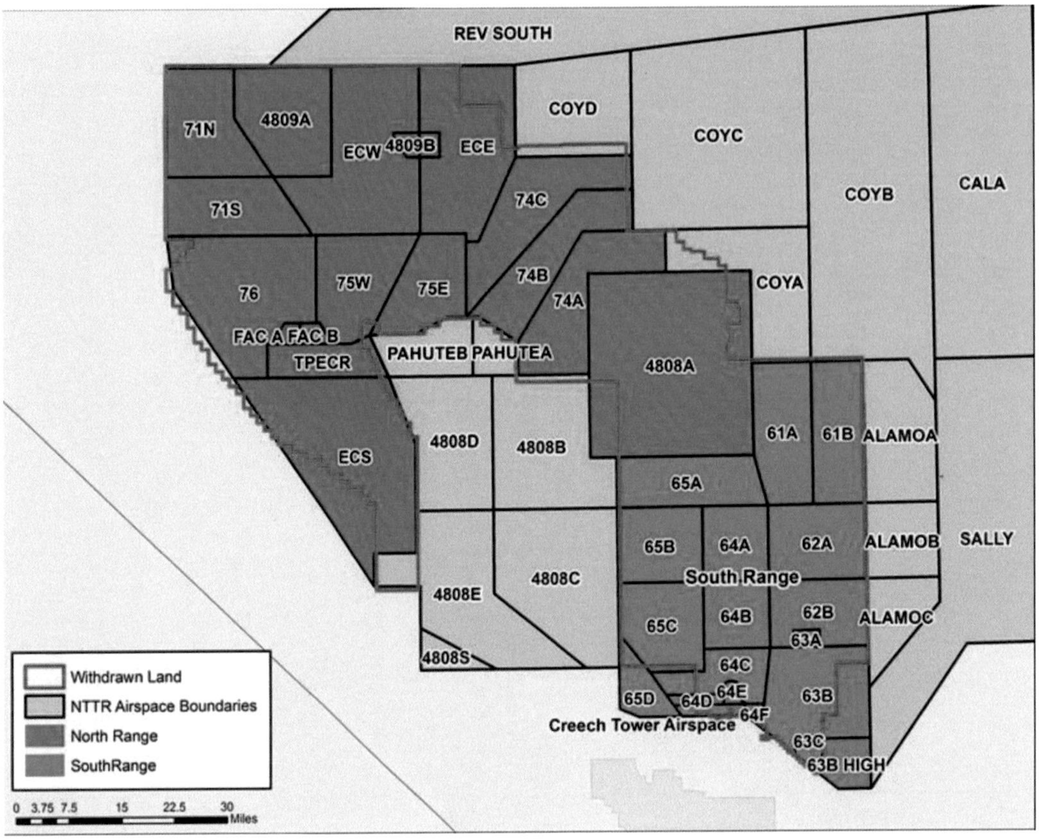

SOURCE: Map created by RAND from 1:800000. U.S. National Atlas Federal and Indian Land Areas, 2010 using ArcGIS. Version 10.1. and ArcGIS data from NTTR.

The orange line in Figure A.4 marks the border of the lands withdrawn for the Air Force. The figure also shows that NTTR is divided into a North Range and a South Range. The North Range has approximately 1.9 million acres, and the South Range approximately one million acres of land.[70]

Airspace and Air Force-Withdrawn Land

An interesting aspect of Figure A.4 is the varying amount of overlap of the airspace boundaries with the withdrawn land boundaries. For many of the restricted areas, such as most of those in the northwest part of the NTTR, all of the land underneath them is withdrawn. For others, such as Range 76, most of the airspace is over withdrawn land, but some is not. There are also restricted areas, such as the three Alamo areas that are above land, that has not been withdrawn. The vast majority of the MOA airspace is over land that has not been withdrawn, though small portions of Coyote A and Coyote D are over withdrawn land. Finally, note that in

---

[70] See Nellis Air Force Base, 2009, for the sizes of the North and South Ranges.

the western part of the NTTR, some withdrawn land is outside the airspace boundaries. These varying intersections become more interesting when the different organizations responsible for land management are considered.

NTTR Land Management

As the *2011 NTTR Comprehensive Range Plan* states, "land management of the NTTR is a complex relationship."[71] This is because there are at least five parties involved in management of the lands under NTTR airspace:

- The Air Force
- The Department of Energy (DOE)
- USFWS
- BLM
- State of Nevada

Figure A.5 shows the areas for which these organizations are responsible.

[71] Nellis Air Force Base, 2011, p. 45.

Figure A.5. Land Ownership in the NTTR

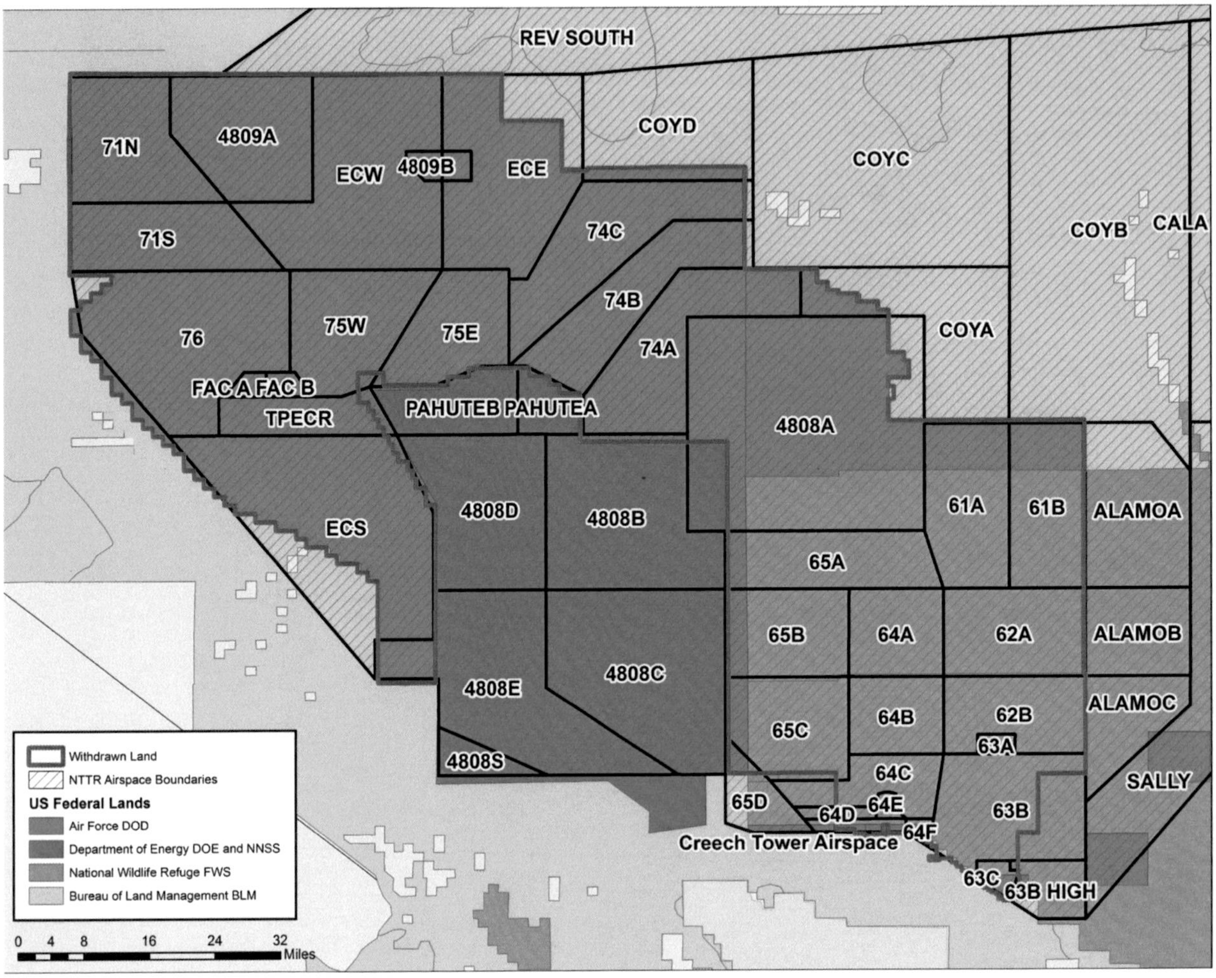

SOURCE: Map created by RAND from 1:800000. U.S. National Atlas Federal and Indian Land Areas, 2010 using ArcGIS. Version 10.1. and ArcGIS data from NTTR

Nevada National Security Site

Note the large amount of land between the north and south ranges under the R-4808 restricted area and the Pahute area (which is under R-4807) that is not withdrawn for the Air Force. This land has been withdrawn for the Department of Energy as part of the Nevada National Security Site (NNSS), which is part of the National Nuclear Security Administration.[72]

According to the Defense Nuclear Facilities Board, the NNSS (formerly the Nevada Test Site) is "an extensive outdoor laboratory and national experiment center located in southern

[72] Land was withdrawn for the NNSS by a series of Public Land Orders. See Nevada Division of Environmental Protection, *Federal Facility Agreement and Consent Order (FFACO), Appendix I, Description of Facilities, Revision No. 4*, February 2008. In addition, Public Law 106-65 transferred the Pahute Mesa area to DOE control. According to a February 19, 2014 email from the Nevada Field Counsel at NNSS, the language for this transfer is understood to mean that the Pahute Mesa withdrawal is permanent, and will not come up for renewal.

Nevada, about 75 miles northwest of Las Vegas. Activities at the site include preparations for the disposition of damaged nuclear weapons, subcritical experiments, criticality experiments, emergency response training, and waste management."[73] It contains about 1,360 square miles of desert mountainous terrain similar to the land withdrawn for the NTTR. It supports national security, homeland security initiatives, waste management, environment restoration, and defense and non-defense research and development for DOE/NNSA, and other government entities.[74]

BLM Land

The orange border in Figure A.5 defines the area of land that has been withdrawn for the NTTR. The green area represents the area withdrawn for the NNSS. As noted above, some airspace in the North Range is not over withdrawn land; Figure A.5 shows this land in light orange, which means that BLM manages it. A small sliver of land under area 65D in the South Range also is under BLM management. The BLM manages the North Range's Nevada Wild Horse Range.

In accordance with various laws, the NTTR developed an RMP and Environmental Impact Statement in 2001, which was approved in a Record of Decision (ROD) that was released in 2004.[75] NTTR interprets the ROD as saying that the entire NTTR will be closed to non-military uses and the general public. BLM may manage wildlife and wildlife habitat according to their Resource Management Plan as long as resource management activities do not impact the military mission. In addition, BLM's responsibilities include:

- Management of the wild horse according to the resource management plan (RMP) ROD
- Protecting unique habitats for threatened and endangered species as well as the military mission
- Protecting the desert tortoise
- Controlling any wildfires on NTTR, including DNWR
- Recognizing that all responsibilities are secondary to the military mission.[76]

---

[73] U.S. Defense Nuclear Facilities Safety Board, "Nevada National Security Site," undated. The name of the site was changed from the NTS to NNSS in August 2010 (see U.S. National Nuclear Security Administration, "Nevada National Security Site," fact sheet, August 23, 2010).

[74] U.S. Department of Energy, *Final Site-Wide Environmental Impact Statement for the Continued Operation of the Department of Energy/National Nuclear Security Administration Nevada National Security Site and Off-site Locations in the State of Nevada (NNWS SWEIS)*, Washington D.C.: Office of National Environmental Policy Act (NEPA) Policy and Compliance, DOE/EIS-0426, February 2013, pp. S3–S4.

[75] U.S. Bureau of Land Management, *Record of Decision for the Approved Nevada Test and Training Range Resource Management and Final Environmental Impact Statement*, Las Vegas, Nev.: BLM Las Vegas Field Office, July 2004.

[76] Nellis Air Force Base, 2010, p. 23.

U.S. Fish and Wildlife Service Land

The light olive green-colored area in Figure A.5 is the Desert National Wildlife Refuge (DNWR). This refuge was created by Executive Order in 1936,[77] and is now the largest national wildlife refuge in the continental United States, with more than 1.6 million acres of land. The red border of withdrawn lands shows that about half of the DNWR, approximately 842,254 acres, overlaps the South Range of the NTTR.[78] The Military Lands Withdrawal Act of 1999 directs that the Secretary of the Interior is to manage this portion of the DNWR in coordination with the Secretary of the Air Force, and a memorandum of understanding renewed in 1997 describes how this is to be done.[79] The memorandum allows the Air Force to use about 112,000 acres of DNWR land for air-to-ground targeting, and the Withdrawal Act transferred primary jurisdiction of these impact areas to the Air Force, with the Secretary of the Interior maintaining secondary jurisdiction for wildlife conservation purposes.[80]

In addition to this co-managed land, note that Figure A.5 indicates that a small portion of the DNWR managed by USFWS is in range 65D, which is land that has not been withdrawn for the NTTR. Finally, the Alamo Restricted Areas are over DNWR land that is not included in NTTR withdrawn land.

The 1997 MOU governing management of the shared DNWR land says:

> The [U.S. Fish and Wildlife] Service is the federal agency primarily responsible for the welfare and management of the land, wildlife and other natural resources, and for protection of cultural and archeological resources, and for research thereon in the refuge. The service is also the federal agency with specific responsibilities for protection of threatened and endangered species and management of desert bighorn sheep, desert tortoises and migratory birds.[81]

As a result, NTTR interprets USFWS responsibilities to be:[82]

- Management of natural, cultural and archeological resources on the DNWR
- Conservation of wildlife resources and preservation of the desert bighorn sheep within the DNWR

---

[77] Roosevelt, 1936.

[78] Acreage figure for the overlap is from U.S. Department of the Air Force and U.S. Department of the Interior, 2013 draft.

[79] U.S. Department of the Air Force and U.S. Department of the Interior, 1997.

[80] This is in Section 3011, paragraph (b) (3) of the Act. In a July 2000 "Memorandum of Agreement for the Acquisition of Replacement Property in Nevada" between the Air Force and the USFWS, it was agreed that the Air Force would provide $15 million to USFWS to acquire lands to replace the 112,000 acres. Paragraph (b)(3) and paragraph (b)(5)(f) of Section 3011 of the 1999 Military Lands Withdrawal Act authorize such a transaction. Paragraph (b) (3) and paragraph (b) (5) (f) of Section 3011 of the 1999 Military Lands Withdrawal Act appear to expect such a transaction.

[81] U.S. Department of the Air Force and U.S. Department of the Interior, 1997.

[82] Nellis Air Force Base, 2010, p. 24.

- Protection of federally listed threatened and endangered species and their habitats according to the Endangered Species Act
- Management of the desert bighorn sheep hunt under the direction of Nellis AFB and in cooperation with the Nevada Department of Wildlife
- Assistance to NTTR, under the provisions of the Sikes Act, in managing natural resources by providing expertise on issues related to endangered species, fisheries, invasive species, migratory birds, law enforcement, wetlands, and environmental contaminants.

State of Nevada Interests

While the state of Nevada does not directly manage any of the land in the NTTR, it does have an interest in environmental and public activity issues in the range. For example, there is a Memorandum of Understanding between Nellis AFB and the state regarding the management of bighorn sheep in the Stonewall Mountain area, which is in the western part of the North Range.[83] This MOU includes an agreement that Nellis AFB will attempt to schedule a three-week hunting period during which authorized hunting parties will have access to the area.

In 1997 the Air Force, BLM, DOE, USFWS, and the State of Nevada-Clearinghouse signed a Five-Party Cooperative Agreement that enjoined the signatories to meet at least annually to "foster cooperation, consistency, and collaboration in land and resource management."[84]

---

83 Nellis Air Force Base and State of Nevada, "Memorandum of Understanding Between Nellis Air Force Base and the State of Nevada Regarding Stonewall Mountain Bighorn Sheep Management," July 1997.

84 A copy of the Five-Party Cooperative Agreement can be found in Nellis Air Force Base, *Legislative Environmental Impact Statement for the Renewal of the Nellis Air Force Range Land Withdrawal,* March 1999, Appendix C.

Appendix B. Background on U.S. Wilderness

In this appendix, we provide background information on what wilderness means in terms of U.S. law and federal policy. We describe where wilderness has been designated on federal lands, and its intended and perceived value as wild places. This context is needed to understand why the NTTR has a wilderness consideration; how this impacts operations there; whether NTTR-withdrawn lands within the DNWR area meet the current legal wilderness criteria; and the role that this proposed DNWR wilderness plays in the broader system of federal wilderness lands.

Why Wilderness Was Created and What It Means

Because of increasing "population" and "settlements" and the growth of "mechanization," Congress passed The Wilderness Act of 1964 to preserve and protect lands "in their natural condition."[85] The idea was to protect "some of the most natural and undisturbed places in America" because of "the immediate and lasting benefits of wild places to the human spirit and fabric of our nation."[86] As the act stated: "It is hereby declared to be the policy of Congress to secure for the American people of the present and future generations the benefits of an enduring resource of wilderness."[87]

Wilderness was defined as federal land areas that have not been significantly impacted by man and remain in a nearly natural condition. The official definition:

> A wilderness, in contrast with those areas where man and his own works dominate the landscape, is hereby recognized as an area where the earth and its community of life are untrammeled by man, where man himself is a visitor who does not remain. An area of wilderness is further defined to mean in this chapter an area of underdeveloped Federal land retaining its primeval character and influence, without permanent improvements or human habitation, which is protected and managed so as to preserve its natural conditions and which (1) generally appears to have been affected primarily by the forces of nature, with the imprint of man's work substantially unnoticeable; (2) has outstanding opportunities for solitude or a primitive and unconfined type of recreation; (3) has at least five thousand acres of land or is of sufficient size as to make practicable its preservation and use in an unimpaired condition; and (4) may also contain ecological, geological, or other features of scientific, educational, scenic, or historical value.[88]

---

[85] Public Law 88-577.

[86] U.S. Forest Service, "Wilderness, Wild and Scenic Rivers, and Protected Areas," April 6, 2010.

[87] Public Law 88-577.

[88] Public Law 88-577.

The four parts of this definition are key to understanding what federal lands can be designated as wilderness.

The Wilderness Act also went on to specify what uses were allowed and prohibited in wilderness. "Wilderness areas shall be devoted to the public purposes of recreational, scenic, scientific, educational, conservation, and historical use," it said.[89] This statement is extremely important, because it is the only part of the Wilderness Act that specifies what people may do in wilderness and because these are very general terms. However, the agencies have defined allowable activities to include those preserving the character of the wilderness areas and wilderness experience for current and future generations. Recreation covers human activities such as hiking, jogging, and skiing. It also can include some types of hunting. Scenic activities include bird and other wildlife observation and wildlife and nature painting and photography. Scientific activities include conducting research about the flora, fauna, geology and other natural systems. Educational activities include learning about the wildlife and natural systems within that wilderness. For example, according to the Fish and Wildlife Service, "Wilderness is a place where children can connect with nature and learn about the intricate web of life."[90] Conservation refers to the protection of species, habitat, and the natural environment. Wilderness areas can play an important role in helping to protect habitat for threatened and endangered species (T&ESs) and other species of concern. Sometimes, historical uses of the land are allowed that are inconsistent with wilderness. For example, in some cases, limited motor vehicle use is allowed to support grazing that had been and continues to be allowed on the property.[91] Most of the permitted activities in wilderness areas only are allowed when they do not degrade or interfere with the quality of the wilderness itself, which is why the Wilderness Act also specifies things that are not allowed in wilderness.

Activities that are prohibited in wilderness according to the Wilderness Act include commercial enterprise, the building of roads, structures, and the use of mechanized vehicles because these activities could harm or destroy the fundamental nature of the wilderness. Exceptions are made for area administration and health and safety reasons. Specifically, the Wilderness Act states:

> Except as specifically provided for in this Act, and subject to existing private rights, there shall be no commercial enterprise and no permanent road within any wilderness area designated by this Act and, except as necessary to meet minimum requirements for the administration of the area for the purpose of this Act (including measures required in emergencies involving the health and safety

---

89 Public Law 88-577, Sec. 4(b).

90 U.S. Fish and Wildlife Service, "Welcome to Wilderness In the National Wildlife Refuge System," brochure, undated.

91 U.S. Bureau of Land Management, "Frequently Asked Questions: The Wilderness Idea," updated January 20, 2012.

> of persons within the area), there shall be no temporary road, no use of motor vehicles, motorized equipment or motorboats, no landing of aircraft, no other form of mechanical transport, and no structure or installation within any such area.[92]

Exceptions were made for some of these restricted activities in places where they were already established, such as the use of use of aircraft or motorboats on wilderness lands, which "may be permitted to continue subject to such restrictions as the secretary of Agriculture deems desirable."[93]

Where the Wilderness is Located

The Wilderness Act of 1964 also created a National Wilderness Preservation System (NWPS) on federal lands to identify, preserve and protect these wilderness areas. This National Wilderness Preservation System is

> to be composed of federally owned areas designated by Congress as "wilderness areas," and these shall be administered for the use and enjoyment of the American people in such manner as will leave them unimpaired for future use and enjoyment as wilderness, and so as to provide for the protection of these areas, the preservation of their wilderness character, and for the gathering and dissemination of information regarding their use and enjoyment as wilderness; and no Federal lands shall be designated as "wilderness areas" except as provided for in this chapter or by a subsequent Act.[94]

The creation of this National Wilderness Preservation System was focused on two main federal departments: the Department of Agriculture (USDA) because of the U.S. Forest Service (USFS) lands, and the DOI because of national parks, national monuments, other National Park Service (NPS) lands, National Wildlife Refuges (NWR), and game ranges.

The Wilderness Act directed the secretary of Agriculture or the chief of the Forest Service to designate areas within national forests already classified as "wilderness," "wild," or "canoe" at least 30 days prior to September 3, 1964 as wilderness areas. The Act further directed the secretary of Agriculture to review primitive areas in national forests and the secretary of Interior to review roadless areas in the national park system, national wildlife refuge system, and game ranges for their suitability for preservation as wilderness and report on whether the agency recommends each area as suitable or non-suitable for wilderness preservation within 10 years. Specifically, for the Secretary of the Interior, the act stated:

> Within ten years after September 3, 1964 the Secretary of the Interior shall review every roadless area of five thousand contiguous acres or more in the

[92] Public Law 88-577, Sec. 4(c).

[93] Public Law 88-577, Sec. 4(d)(1).

[94] Public Law 88-577.

> national parks, monuments and other units of the national park system and every such area of, and every roadless island within the national wildlife refuges and game ranges, under his jurisdiction on September 3, 1964 and shall report to the President his recommendation as to the suitability or nonsuitability of each such area or island for preservation as wilderness. The President shall advise the President of the Senate and the Speaker of the House of Representatives of his recommendation with respect to the designation as wilderness of each such area or island on which review has been completed, together with a map thereof and a definition of its boundaries.[95]

This part of the act required DOI staff to examine the DNWR, all other NWRs and game ranges, all national parks, all national monuments, and all other national park system lands to assess what areas might be suitable for wilderness. This land-analysis task was quite significant, especially given the remoteness of some of these areas and the technological and scientific capabilities back in 1964, long before global positioning system (GPS) and geographic information system (GIS) data could be used to help provide accurate maps of the areas. As will be discussed below, the DNWR proposed wilderness analysis was conducted in the early 1970s and the proposal was submitted to Congress in 1974.

After the president reviews any such federal lands considered suitable for wilderness and recommends them for wilderness preservation, Congress must act to officially designate them as wilderness: "A recommendation of the President for designation as wilderness shall become effective only if so provided by an Act of Congress."[96] Any lands that are recommended as suitable for official wilderness status by DOI or USDA are in limbo until Congress officially acts on the request to designate the lands as wilderness.

With the passage of the Wilderness Act in 1964, 54 areas consisting of 9.1 million acres in 13 states were designated as wilderness.[97] Additional tracts of federal land and numerous acres were added to the National Wilderness Preservation System by different acts of Congress during the 50 years since the passage of this original legislation. For example, the Federal Land Policy and Management Act (FLPMA) of 1976 (Section 603) required that the BLM also assess and recommend suitable bureau lands for wilderness designation by Congress. FLPMA designated BLM Management as the fourth federal agency to manage and maintain wilderness lands. In 1980, Congress passed the Alaska National Interest Lands Conservation Act, which added more than 56 million acres of wilderness to the system. The California Desert Protection Act of 1994 established Death Valley National Park, Joshua Tree National Park, and the Mojave National Preserve and added 69 wilderness areas to the National Wilderness Preservation System in the

---

[95] Public Law 88-577.

[96] Public Law 88-577.

[97] University of Montana Department of Forestry and Conservation, Wilderness.net, "The Beginnings of the National Wilderness Preservation System," undated.

California desert,[98] including Death Valley Wilderness totaling 3,102,497 acres (about 3,057,147 acres in California and about 45,350 acres in Nevada).[99] By 2004, the National Wilderness Preservation System included 777 areas (109,511,966 acres) in 44 states and Puerto Rico.[100] California has the most wilderness areas with 149, followed by Arizona with 90, Nevada with 68 and Alaska with 48.[101] However, Alaska has the largest number of acres protected as wilderness with 57,425,992 acres, followed by California with 14,989,637 acres, Idaho with 4,523,215 acres, and Arizona with 4,517,898 acres.[102] Table B.1 shows the total number of acres of wilderness and total number of units of wilderness by state for the states that have more than 1 million acres of wilderness. Nevada has more than 3 million acres of wilderness within the National Wilderness Preservation System.

Table B.1. States with More Than 1 Million Acres of Wilderness

State	Acres	Percent of Total Wilderness Acres	Wilderness Units	Percent of Total Wilderness Units
Alaska	57,425,992	52	48	6
California	14,989,637	14	149	19
Idaho	4,523,215	4	12	2
Arizona	4,517,898	4	90	12
Washington	4,462,822	4	31	4
Colorado	3,699,309	3	43	6
Montana	3,443,407	3	15	2
Nevada	3,372,418	3	68	9
Wyoming	3,111,232	3	15	2
Oregon	2,474,435	2	47	6
New Mexico	1,650,596	2	25	3
Florida	1,422,247	1	17	2
Utah	1,160,331	1	33	4

SOURCE: University of Montana Department of Forestry and Conservation, Wilderness.net, "Number of Wilderness Units By State" and "Wilderness Acreage By State."

Other federal lands also could potentially become wilderness. USDA and DOI agencies have designated many of these land areas as Wilderness Study Areas (WSA). They are defined as federal lands that "contain undeveloped lands that retain their primeval character without human habitation, and are managed to preserve their natural character until congress acts to either

---

[98] Public Law 103-433, California Desert Protection Act, October 31, 1994.

[99] University of Montana Department of Forestry and Conservation, Wilderness.net, "Death Valley Wilderness," undated.

[100] University of Montana Department of Forestry and Conservation, Wilderness.net, "Number of Wilderness Units By State" and "Wilderness Acreage By State," last updated May 29, 2015.

[101] University of Montana Department of Forestry and Conservation, Wilderness.net, "Wilderness Statistics Reports."

[102] University of Montana Department of Forestry and Conservation Wilderness.net, "Wilderness Acreage By State (States with most acreage listed first)."

designate these lands as wilderness or remove the protective management."[103] More specifically, they must meet the wilderness criteria as spelled out by the Wilderness Act of 1964. WSAs have been reviewed as potential wilderness, but require further study before they can be submitted as recommended or proposed wilderness. WSAs are BLM, USFWS National Refuge System and National Forest System land areas "designated by Congress for further study before final designation as wilderness." USFWS' WSAs

> are identified and established through the inventory component of a Wilderness review and include all areas that are still undergoing the Wilderness review process. These lands are managed in the same manner as designated wilderness, so that, if they become wilderness, their Wilderness character is preserved.[104]

BLM manages more than 545 Wilderness Study Areas (WSAs) consisting of almost 12.7 million acres located in the Western states and Alaska. "Until Congress makes a final determination on a WSA, the BLM manages these areas to preserve their suitability for designation as wilderness."[105] As these BLM and USFWS examples illustrate, WSAs are managed as *de facto* wilderness until Congress decides their future..

Over the years, Congress and federal agencies have protected other natural areas for the public to enjoy that have some qualities similar to wilderness areas, though they are not classified as official wilderness areas. For example, in 1968, Congress passed the Wild and Scenic Rivers Act "to strike a balance between the demands for hydropower, flood control, and irrigation with the need to protect our most outstandingly remarkable rivers."[106] Such river areas are designated as wild, scenic or recreational rivers, and "protect outstanding natural, cultural and recreational values."[107] Parts of these wild and scenic rivers can have attributes that are close to wilderness values, such as areas for solitude and primitive recreation. Similar to the Wilderness Act, this "legislation ensures free-flowing waterways for the benefit and enjoyment of present and future generations."[108] Similarly,

> National Scenic and Historic Trails, National Historic Landmarks, Volcanic Monuments, Scenic Areas, Recreation Areas, Preserves, and Monuments are among additional designations bestowed by Congress to ensure protection of unique natural, cultural and recreational values. Collectively, Wildernesses, Wild and Scenic Rivers, National Scenic and Historic Trails and other Congressionally Designated Areas comprise almost a quarter of all lands managed by the Forest

---

[103] U.S. Bureau of Land Management, "Wilderness Study Areas," April 3, 2013.

[104] University of Montana Department of Forestry and Conservation, Wilderness.net, "Land Classifications Related to Wilderness," undated.

[105] U.S. Bureau of Land Management, 2013.

[106] U.S. Forest Service, "Wilderness, Wild and Scenic Rivers, and Protected Areas," April 6, 2010.

[107] U.S. Forest Service, "Wild and Scenic Rivers," November 1, 2007.

[108] U.S. Forest Service, 2010.

Service and afford permanent protection to some of the most varied, ecologically significant, and valued federal lands and free flowing waters in the nation.[109]

Thus, national trail systems and recreation areas as well as national parks and monuments provide some similar recreation benefits as found in wilderness areas.

DOI also manages many land areas that have wilderness qualities, such as parts of some national parks, national monuments, and national wildlife refuges.

Value of Wilderness

Since the passage of the original Wilderness Act, the public importance and value of these wilderness areas has grown. The Wilderness Act mentioned some of these values; others have been assessed over time by surveys of the American public and research studies about the benefits of wilderness.

Wilderness has a range of direct and indirect benefits and values to the public and society. Direct values occur when people have direct contact with wilderness areas, such as with recreation. Indirect values occur without direct contact, such as someone valuing the existence of wilderness. We have grouped the wilderness benefits into 10 main areas:

1. Recreational
2. Ecological
3. Educational
4. Scientific
5. Historical and cultural
6. Scenic and aesthetic
7. Geological
8. Economic
9. Spiritual
10. Existence, bequest and option

The first six wilderness value areas were mentioned in the Wilderness Act as purposes of wilderness: "Wilderness areas shall be devoted to the public purposes of recreational, scenic, scientific, educational, conservation, and historical use."[110] The other benefits have come from public surveys and the literature on wilderness values. However, the original Wilderness Act implied most of these values. In the early 1960s, wilderness was, and it remains, a part of American culture and identity. The well-known Pulitzer Prize winning author and conservationist Wallace Stegner in 1960 wrote a famous letter to the Outdoor Recreation Resources Review Commission that was instrumental in the development of the Wilderness Act.

---

[109] U.S. Forest Service, 2010.

[110] Public Law 88-577, Sec. 4(b).

In this letter, Stegner describes the importance of wilderness and how it shaped Americans as democratic individuals:

> I want to speak for the wilderness idea as something that has helped form our character and that has certainly shaped our history as a people. … To make such a man, such a democrat, such a believer in human individual dignity, as Mark Twain himself, the frontier was necessary, Hannibal and the Mississippi and Virginia City, and reaching out from those the wilderness; the wilderness as opportunity and idea, the thing that has helped to make an American different from and, until we forget it in the roar of our industrial cities, more fortunate than other men. For an American, insofar as he is new and different at all, is a civilized man who has renewed himself in the wild. The American experience has been the confrontation by old peoples and cultures of a world as new as if it had just risen from the sea. That gave us our hope and our excitement, and the hope and excitement can be passed on to newer Americans, Americans who never saw any phase of the frontier. But only so long as we keep the remainder of our wild as a reserve and a promise—a sort of wilderness bank.[111]

Stegner presented an esoteric and even a philosophical rationale for preserving wilderness in the early 1960s. Here, we take an approach to explaining the value of wilderness that is found in the literature today, by briefly describing each of the 10 benefit areas. It is important to understand the different types of benefits that different wilderness lands can provide, because if a major part of the NTTR portion of the DNWR currently meets the criteria for wilderness as it was proposed in 1974, it is logical to ask what value it provides to the country as wilderness.

1. Recreation benefits. Wilderness provides a wide range of recreation benefits. Americans hike, backpack, camp, climb mountains, bird-watch and view other wildlife, canoe, raft, star gaze, and take pictures in wilderness areas. In fact, on average, people take between 16 million and 35 million trips to wilderness each year for such activities.[112] Contrary to a common misconception, people also are able to hunt and fish in wilderness areas. For instance, hunters hunt bighorn sheep in the proposed wilderness areas of the DNWR. According to the "2011 National Survey of Fishing, Hunting, and Wildlife-Associated Recreation," which the U.S. Census Bureau conducted for USFWS, Americans' participation in wildlife-related recreation is high. The survey found that more than 90 million U.S. residents who were at least 16 years of age participated in wildlife-related recreation in 2011, including 33.1 million people who fished, 13.7 million who hunted, and 71.8 million who participated in at least one wildlife-watching activity (observing, feeding, or photographing wildlife). This was a 3 percent increase from

[111] Wallace Stegner, "Wilderness Letter," to David E. Peterson of the Outdoor Recreation Resources Review Commission, Berkeley, Calif., December 3, 1960.

[112] H. Ken Cordell, John C. Bergstrom, and J.M. Bowker, *The Multiple Values of Wilderness*, State College, Pa.: Venture Publishing, 2005.

2006, mostly from the number of people who fished and hunted.[113] Obviously, many of these activities were conducted in non-wilderness areas. However, the point of these statistics is to show how Americans value wildlife-related recreation activities that can be conducted in wilderness areas, such as hunting and wildlife viewing, and that participation is strong.

2. Ecological benefits. Wilderness provides a range of environmental benefits to U.S. water, air, and wildlife. Wilderness helps protect water supplies, improves water quality and has other water-management benefits. A main benefit of wilderness in many forested areas is to help provide watershed and water quality protection. For example, wilderness in Shenandoah National Park helps protect water quality for Washington D.C. and some of nearby Northern Virginia because 40 percent of the park has received a wilderness designation.[114] This includes the Big Run watershed whose waters flow into the Shenandoah River, which flows into the Potomac River, a drinking water source for Washington D.C. and parts of Northern Virginia. Some wilderness areas, such as the Great Swamp National Wildlife Refuge Wilderness in New Jersey, help with flood control, groundwater recharge, and storm water detention and filtration. Local tributaries contribute waters to this swamp that contain both natural and synthetic pollutants, and the swamp serves as an important nutrient and sediment sink for these pollutants.[115]

Wilderness areas help provide clean air quality and protect airsheds. The Clean Air Act (CAA) created the Prevention of Significant Deterioration (PSD) permitting program to prevent significant deterioration of air quality in areas where air quality is better than the national standards established by the U.S. Environmental Protection Agency (EPA) to protect public health and welfare. One of the purposes of the PSD program is "to preserve, protect, and enhance the air quality in national parks, national wilderness areas, national monuments, national seashores, and other areas of special natural, recreational, scenic, or historic value." "Congress gave the greatest degree of air quality protection to certain national parks and wilderness areas. These "Class I" areas are national parks or national wilderness areas that were so designated as of August 7, 1977, and that are greater than 6,000 acres (parks) or 5,000 acres (wilderness)."[116] By protecting air quality in these wilderness areas, it helps improve air quality of an entire airshed.

---

[113] Note that some people participated in more than one wildlife-related recreation activity, such as hunting and fishing, which is why the total number of participants is not the sum of each activity type. The Census Bureau has conducted this survey every five years for multiple decades for USFWS. (U.S. Fish and Wildlife Service, "2011 National Survey of Fishing, Hunting, and Wildlife-Associated Recreation," September 2013, pp. 4-5.)

[114] National Park Service, "Shenandoah National Park: Wilderness," updated December 11, 2013.

[115] Ten Towns Great Swamp Watershed Management Committee, "Great Swamp Watershed Water Quality Monitoring Report," March 2, 2007.

[116] U.S. Fish and Wildlife Service, "National Wildlife Refuge System: Permit Applications," updated March 19, 2013.

Wilderness provides wildlife habitat and species conservation. Many wilderness areas provide nesting and wintering grounds for a range of bird species and stopover areas for migratory neotropical birds. They also provide habitat for large mammals that need large tracts of undisturbed land; such species include grizzly bears, wolves, elk moose, wolverine and moose. For instance, grizzly bears in Yellowstone National Park, Grand Tetons National Park and the surrounding national forests which make up the Greater Yellowstone Ecosystem (GYE) are estimated to have average home ranges for males and females of 874 km^2 and 281 km^2 respectively.[117] Within Yellowstone National Park, slightly more than 2 million of the park's total 2.2 million acres are Recommended Wilderness" and managed as wilderness according to the Wilderness Act.[118] These "Recommended Wilderness" areas provide important habitat for grizzly bears.

Wilderness provides habitat for fish and game species. For instance, the Golden Trout Wilderness consists of 303,511 acres and is located in the Sierra Nevada, in Tulare County and Inyo County, Calif. This wilderness area helps protect the state fish, the golden trout, a popular fishing species that has been declining in its natural habitat.[119] The proposed wilderness areas within the DNWR provide habitat for bighorn sheep, a big-game species.

Wilderness areas also help conserve biodiversity and habitat for threatened and endangered species (T&ES). For instance, several wilderness areas in California and Nevada help provide habitat and protection for the threatened desert tortoise. In fact, at the Piute Mountains Wilderness, "the entire wilderness area has been identified as critical habitat for the desert tortoise."[120] The Delamar Mountains Wilderness, consisting of 111,066 acres in southern Lincoln County, Nevada also provides some "critical habitat" for the desert tortoise.[121] In Florida, the Florida Keys Wilderness (located in part of the National Key Deer Refuge and the Key West and Great White Heron National Wildlife Refuges) provides habitat for at least 22 federal and/or state threatened and endangered species, including the Key Deer, Loggerhead Turtle, Atlantic

---

[117] Melissa Reed-Eckert, "Species Assessment for Grizzly (Brown) Bear (Ursus Arctos) in Wyoming," Cheyenne, Wyo.: BLM Wyoming State Office, September 2004, p. 15.

[118] It is interesting to note that Yellowstone National Park was recommended for wilderness designation in 1972. Like the DNWR proposed wilderness areas, Congress has yet to act to designate these "Recommended Wilderness" areas as official wilderness. (Yellowstone National Park, "Yellowstone Wilderness," updated December 12, 2013.)

[119] University of Montana Department of Forestry and Conservation, Wilderness.net, "Golden Trout Wilderness," undated.

[120] University of Montana Department of Forestry and Conservation, Wilderness.net, "Piute Mountains Wilderness," undated.

[121] University of Montana Department of Forestry and Conservation, Wilderness.net, "Delamar Mountains Wilderness," undated.

Green Turtle, Miami blue butterfly, Garber's spurge, Lower Keys marsh rabbit, and Piping Plover; as well as nine federal candidate species.[122]

Wilderness areas also help address climate change, often by providing carbon sequestration. For example, "Mature, fully stocked forests sequester carbon to help slow the process of global warming."[123]

3. Educational Benefits. Wilderness also provides educational benefits for college, university, and primary and secondary students as well as community groups, such as Boy Scout and Girl Scout troops. Wilderness areas are used as outdoor classrooms and for experimental learning to teach about science and the environment. For instance, the Teton Science School, which has campuses in Grand Teton National Park and Jackson, Wyo., provides nature and environmental science classes and summer camps for children and adults in wilderness and other natural areas of the Greater Yellowstone Ecosystem.[124] Wilderness areas also are used to help teach outdoor recreation related skills such as navigation, tracking, outdoor living and survival skills. Some students also learn the importance of environmental stewardship and a land ethic.

Wilderness areas are used to help provide personal growth, therapy and healing. Groups like Outward Bound[125] and Wildlinks[126] have wilderness treatment programs to help adults and youth deal with physical disabilities, illness, substance abuse, problematic behaviors, psychological problems, death of a loved one, and other major life challenges through outdoor recreation activities in wilderness and other natural areas. For example, Outward Bound has a program called Intercept which includes wilderness expeditions to help struggling teens and at-risk youth who are starting to demonstrate destructive behaviors.[127] Many of these wilderness and other outdoor recreation programs are being used successfully across the United States to help adults and youth. One study found that "wilderness and expeditionary courses are well-suited to teach outdoor skills, self-confidence in general and confidence specifically during adversity, changes

---

[122] Molly McCarter, "Florida Keys Wilderness: A Report on Wilderness Character Monitoring," U.S. Fish and Wildlife Service: National Key Deer, Key West, and Great White Heron National Wildlife Refuges, August 2012.

[123] The Wilderness Society, "The Economic Benefits of Wilderness: Focus on Property Value Enhancement," Ecology and Economics Research Department's *Science & Policy Brief*, March 2004.

[124] For more information, see Teton Science Schools, "Teton Science Schools connects people, nature and place through education, science and stewardship," undated.

[125] Outward Bound is a system of schools dedicated to helping people learn through challenging experiences so they can grow individually as well as become more active in their communities. They provide schools in wilderness settings and urban communities, and place students in physically and mentally challenging situations to help them discover self-confidence, physical and mental strength and a compassion for others.

[126] WildLink gives underserved high school teens in California a series of wilderness- and home-based experiences that help them to better their own lives and their communities. See WildLink, "About Us," undated.

[127] Outward Bound, "Intercept for Struggling Youth," undated.

in life perspectives, group leadership skills, an appreciation for nature, and teamwork."[128] The military also uses wilderness areas and outdoor activities to help provide similar benefits for servicemen/women and veterans. For instance, the Army uses high adventure outdoor activities in natural areas, which sometimes include wilderness areas, in its Warrior Adventure Quest (WAQ) Program. The WAQ Program provides supervised, high-adventure activities for platoon-sized units that have returned from deployment. Benefits from the program include building unit cohesion, strengthening soldier resiliency, reducing stress, mitigating common high-risk behaviors, and increasing physical activity.[129]

4. Scientific Benefits. Wilderness also provides value to scientists in understanding natural environments and phenomena, from studying climate change impacts to analyzing invasive species patterns to tracking migratory birds. Biological research about the spread of invasive species and diseases in wilderness contribute to science but also can have important implications for agriculture and forestry. Wilderness areas provide pristine laboratories to study these issues. Often wilderness serves as "the control by which scientists can judge the impacts of management on other parts of the landscape."[130] For example, scientists have studied the spread and removal of salt cedar (tamaric) in California wilderness areas. Salt cedar is a problematic invasive species, which has impacted many desert areas by sucking up scarce water supplies and displacing native species. Wilderness areas also provide natural laboratories for studying species and their habitats. In addition, monitoring elusive species like grizzly bears and bighorn sheep in such natural environments helps biologists learn more about how these species live. For instance, within the Cabeza Prieta Wilderness encompassing more than 90 percent of the Cabeza Prieta National Wildlife Refuge in Arizona's Sonoran desert, scientists monitor the desert bighorn sheep and endangered Sonoran pronghorn antelope populations.[131] Wilderness areas also have been studied to better understand the phenomena, effects and recovery from fire, floods and earthquakes. For example, consider the research conducted since the tremendous wildfires at Yellowstone National Park in 1988 when more than 793,000 acres burned, about 36 percent of the park, much of this in proposed wilderness areas.[132] Scientists have learned a great amount by studying the effects of fire size and patterns on post-fire vegetation and ecosystem processes,

---

[128] Jim Sibthorp, Nathan Furman, Karen Paisley and John Gookin, "Long-term Impacts Attributed to Participation in Adventure Education: Preliminary Findings from NOLS," *Research in Outdoor Education*, Volume 9, 2008.

[129] For a sample of classes and more information about the WAQ Program see Fort Bragg Morale, Welfare and Recreation Program, "Warrior Adventure Quest," undated.

[130] The Wilderness Society, 2004.

[131] For more information on some of the efforts to monitor the endangered Sonoran pronghorn, see Ron Dungan, "Project near Ajo gives pronghorns second chance," *Arizona Republic*, February 6, 2010.

[132] Yellowstone National Park, "History of Wildland Fire in Yellowstone," December 2013.

such as how quickly lodgepole pines grew back.[133] Researchers have estimated that science research conducted on or based on wilderness areas provide an annual estimated economic benefit of $5 million annually.[134]

5. Historical and cultural benefits. Wilderness provides benefits by protecting and preserving historical and cultural sites. Archaeological resources and sites, such as cave paintings, burial grounds, historic cemeteries, and homestead cabins, can be found in wilderness areas. For example, the 29,261 acres of Oregon Badlands Wilderness, located about 12 miles east of Bend, Ore., on BLM lands, contains Native American pictographs. In Southern Nevada, several wilderness areas protect Native American cultural sites and artifacts. The La Madre Mountain Wilderness in Clark County has archaeological sites which include rock art (pictographs and petroglyphs), agave roasting pits, camp sites, rock shelters, and ceramic scatters. Its Brownstone Canyon Archaeological District is listed on the National Register of Historic Places because of the large number and diversity of cultural sites.[135] Similarly, at the Muddy Mountains Wilderness area (also in Clark County) one can find "rock art panels, agave roasting pits, rock shelters, stone flakes, and pot shards."[136] The proposed wilderness in the USFWS public access part of the DNWR near Cow Camp Road contains a Native American rock shelter and agave roasting pits.[137] In addition, wilderness is important to present-day cultures, especially Native Americans.

6. Scenic and aesthetic benefits. Wilderness areas provide value by protecting magnificent scenery, natural landscapes and other scenic and aesthetically appealing areas. For example, the Muddy Mountains Wilderness in Nevada protects scenic and "stunning and colorful sandstone outcrops" and a "magnificent range of rugged limestone cliffs and canyons,"[138] while the Aravaipa Canyon Wilderness in the Sonoran Desert protects the 11-mile long scenic Aravaipa Canyon in southeastern Arizona[139] and the Yosemite Wilderness in California protects spectacular views of El Capitan and other mountains.[140] Many Americans value wilderness for providing such benefits. In fact, in the 2006-2007 National Survey on Recreation and the

---

[133] For more information about this research see: Monica G. Turner, "Fire, vegetation and ecosystem processes in Yellowstone National Park," Madison, Wisc.: University of Wisconsin Department of Zoology, Ecosystem and Landscape Ecology Lab, undated.

[134] John B. Loomis and Robert Richardson, "Economic Values of the U.S. . Wilderness System: Research Evidence to Date and Questions for the Future," *International Journal of Wilderness*, Volume 7, Number 1, April 2001.

[135] Birdandhike.com, "La Madre Mountains Wilderness Area," updated March 29, 2013.

[136] Birdandhike.com, "Muddy Mountains Wilderness Area," updated May 24, 2011.

[137] Birdandhike.com, "Cow Camp Road," updated October 28, 2012.

[138] U.S. Bureau of Land Management, "Muddy Mountains Wilderness," fact sheet, undated.

[139] U.S. Bureau of Land Management, *Aravaipa Canyon: Wilderness Management Plan*, updated July 31, 2013.

[140] University of Montana Department of Forestry and Conservation, Wilderness.net, "Yosemite Wilderness," undated.

Environment (NSRE),[141] 76.5 percent of the respondents, U.S. residents age 16 years or older, said that "providing scenic beauty" was an extremely or very important wilderness value.[142]

7. Geological values. Wilderness areas also were created and have value for preserving and protecting areas of geological significance including caves, volcanoes, canyons, geysers, mountains, fossils, glaciers and beaches. For example, within the Red River Gorge Geological Area of Daniel Boone National Forest in Kentucky is the Clifty Wilderness, which protects 12,646 acres of rugged forest landscape with scenic rock features, including sandstone arches and towering cliffs.[143] Within Badlands National Park in South Dakota, more than one-quarter (64,144 acres) is the Badlands Wilderness. It was designated as wilderness by Congress in 1976. This Badlands Wilderness protects "a moonscape of cliffs, gorges, mesas, soaring spires, keen-edged ridges, and fossil-filled canyons."[144]

8. Economic benefits. Wilderness areas have been found to provide a range of economic benefits. They benefit local economies by providing tourism dollars, increasing property values, and providing ecological services (such as helping to filter and clean water supplies). The tourism dollars benefit local, regional, and national businesses, and come from people who visit wilderness. Such visitors' expenditures include money for airline flights, rental cars, tour guides, hotels, food, equipment, and supplies. According to the "2011 National Survey of Fishing, Hunting, and Wildlife-Associated Recreation," Americans spent $144.7 billion on hunting, fishing, and wildlife-watching activities that year, of which $49.5 billion was trip related and $70.4 billion was spent on equipment. Such activities were conducted in wilderness and other natural areas within the United States. Outdoor recreation businesses are one of the main beneficiaries of such recreation activities in wilderness and other natural areas. In 2006, according to a non-profit group's study, outdoor recreation businesses that supply equipment, supplies, and guides for activities such as camping, hiking, climbing, hunting, fishing, bicycling, snow sports, and wildlife viewing provided 6.1 million jobs and contributed $730 billion to the U.S. economy for the year and $88 billion in annual state and national tax revenue.[145]

Different studies also have found that businesses and people like to settle in counties with wilderness and that property values tend to rise. Businesses will locate in areas near wilderness

---

[141] The National Survey on Recreation and the Environment (NSRE) represents the continuation of the ongoing National Recreation Survey (NRS) series. Begun in 1960 by the congressionally created Outdoor Recreation Resources Review Commission (ORRRC), the first NRS was a four-season, in-the-home survey of outdoor recreation participation in the United States. This survey normally has been conducted about every five to six years since then and includes questions about wilderness and the NWPS.

[142] H. Ken Cordell, Carter J. Betz, Becky Stephens, Shela Mou, and Gary T. Green, "How Do Americans View Wilderness?" U.S. Forest Service, Internet Research Information Series, January 2008.

[143] Daniel Boone National Forest, "Red River Gorge Geological Area," undated.

[144] University of Montana Department of Forestry and Conservation, Wilderness.Net, "Badlands Wilderness," undated.

[145] Outdoor Industry Foundation, "The Active Outdoor Recreation Economy," Boulder, Colo., Fall 2006.

and other protected natural areas, creating more jobs and helping the local economy. For instance, one study of business location decision-making found that businesses ranked scenic beauty, desire for a rural setting, and outdoor recreation opportunities higher than labor costs and tax incentives as reasons for locating in areas providing protected landscapes.[146] One survey of people living in 11 fast-growing counties across the United States found that 45 percent of long-time residents and 60 percent of the new residents in the counties that contained wilderness indicated that the wilderness areas were an important reason for living in those counties.[147]

Other studies have found that property values go up near wilderness and other protected natural areas. In Vermont, a study found that the per-acre price of residential land near Green Mountain National Forest was almost 19 percent higher in towns containing wilderness areas, and land prices fell by about 0.33 percent for each additional kilometer in distance from the closest wilderness boundary.[148] Another study found that owning a home near a NWR, many of which include wilderness areas, had increased property values and helped support the nearby communities' tax base. This study examined home values for urban areas in the Southeast, the Northeast, and the California/Nevada region. The researchers found that owning a home near a national wildlife refuge increased home values by 7 to 9 percent in the Southeast, 4 to5 percent in the Northeast, and 3 to 6 percent in the California/Nevada region.[149]

Ecological services besides helping the environment also provide a range of economic benefits. For example, researchers have estimated the value of federal wilderness areas for watershed protection, carbon storage for climate regulation and the filtering of air and water at between $2 billion and $3.4 billion per year.[150]

9. Spiritual value. Many Americans also enjoy spiritual benefits from wilderness areas through religious and other spiritual experiences in wilderness areas. As the writer Loren Eiseley stated: "It is a commonplace of all religious thought, even the most primitive, that the man seeking visions and insight must go apart from his fellows and live for a time in the wilderness." This quotation shows how the spiritual value of wilderness is also reflected in U.S. literature and by famous nature writers, as Wallace Stegner also did in his 1960 "Wilderness Letter:"

---

146 Jerry D. Johnson and Raymond Rasker, "The Role of Economic and Quality of Life Values in Rural Business Location," *Journal of Rural Studies* Vol. 11, Issue 4, 1995.

147 Gundars Rudzitis and Harley E. Johansen, "How Important is Wilderness? Results from a United States Survey," *Environmental Management*, Vol. 15, Issue 2, 1991.

148 Spencer R. Phillips, "Windfalls for Wilderness: Land Protection and Land Value in the Green Mountains," Virginia Polytechnic Institute & State University doctoral dissertation, UMI No. 3241159, February 4, 2004.

149 Laura O. Taylor, Xiangping Liu and Timothy L. Hamilton, "Amenity Values of Proximity to National Wildlife Refuges," Raleigh, N.C.: North Carolina State University Center for Environmental and Resource Economic Policy, April 2012.

150 Loomis and Richardson, 2001.

> We need to demonstrate our acceptance of the natural world, including ourselves; we need the spiritual refreshment that being natural can produce. And one of the best places for us to get that is in the wilderness where the fun houses, the bulldozers, and the pavement of our civilization are shut out.[151]

Surveys have also shown that Americans value wilderness for its spiritual benefits. In the 2006-2007 National Survey on Recreation and the Environment (NSRE), 57.8 percent of the respondents, U.S. residents age 16 or older, said that "providing spiritual inspiration" was an extremely or very important wilderness value.[152]

10. Existence, bequest and option values. Wilderness areas also can have what are called indirect values or passive-use values, which include existence, bequest, option, and intrinsic benefits. Existence values are those benefits that people place on wilderness just by knowing wilderness exists independent of visiting the areas or any other type of direct use. Valuing the existence of wilderness has become part of the American culture and is reflected in our literature. Many famous conservationists, environmentalists, and nature writers have written about the existence, as well as other values of wilderness. For instance, existence value is demonstrated by a quotation from the nature writer and environmentalist Edward Abbey in *Desert Solitaire:*

> A man could be a lover and defender of wilderness without ever in his lifetime leaving the boundaries of asphalt, powerlines, and right-angled surfaces. We need wilderness whether or not we ever set foot in it. We need a refuge even though we may never need to go there. I may never in my life get to Alaska, for example, but I am grateful that it's there. We need the possibility of escape as surely as we need hope; without it the life of the cities would drive all men into crime or drugs or psychoanalysis.[153]

Bequest value means the value from the ability to pass wilderness on to future generations.. Option values refer to what it is worth to preserve the option of future use of wilderness, namely, opportunities for one to enjoy wilderness in the future. "Intrinsic values are wilderness qualities that exist regardless of human existence."[154]

These indirect values of wilderness also are important to many Americans. For instance, in the 2006-2007 National Survey on Recreation and the Environment, 76.2 percent of the respondents, who were U.S. residents age 16 years or older, said that "Having option to visit wilderness areas in future" was an extremely or very important wilderness value. Meanwhile, 75.7 percent stated "knowing that wilderness areas exist" was an extremely or very important wilderness value.[155]

---

151 Stegner, 1960.

152 Cordell *et al*, 2008.

153 Edward Abbey, *Desert Solitaire*, New York: Ballantine Books, 1968, pp. 148-149.

154 University of Montana Department of Forestry and Conservation, Wilderness.Net, "How Wilderness Benefits You," undated.

155 Cordell *et al*, 2008.

Appendix C. Background on the National Wildlife Refuge System and the Desert National Wildlife Refuge (DNWR)

In this appendix, we provide background information on the National Wildlife Refuge System (NWRS) and how such lands are managed. We also describe basic information about the Desert National Wildlife Refuge, the DNWR wilderness proposal, the current status of the wilderness proposal, and NWR wilderness management processes.

The U.S. National Wildlife Refuge System

The National Wildlife Refuge System originally was developed to protect wildlife by protecting federal lands and waterways that provide important habitat for different wildlife species. According to USFWS:

> The Mission of the National Wildlife Refuge System is to administer a national network of lands and waters for the conservation, management, and where appropriate, restoration of the fish, wildlife, and plant resources and their habitats within the United States for the benefit of present and future generations of Americans.[156]

The National Wildlife Refuge System is managed by USFWS, an agency within the DOI. President Theodore Roosevelt designated Florida's Pelican Island as the first wildlife refuge in 1903.Since then, the National Wildlife Refuge System has grown and by April 2013 included "more than 560 refuges, 38 wetland management districts and other protected areas encompassing 150 million acres of land and water from the Caribbean to the remote Pacific."[157] Every U.S. state and territory has at least one national wildlife refuge; most are within about an hour's drive of large metropolitan areas.

The Refuge Improvement Act of 1997 required all national wildlife refuges in the lower 48 states to develop a CCP by the end of 2012. This act also required "that refuges be managed in a way that ensures the long-term conservation of fish, wildlife, plants, and their habitats and provides for compatible wildlife-dependent recreation."[158] A CCP provides the framework for management decisions on a national wildlife refuge for a 10- to 15-year period, and it undergoes a public review process. The objectives of a CCP are to:

---

[156] U.S. Fish and Wildlife Service, "National Wildlife Refuge System Mission Statement," July 11, 2014.

[157] U.S. Fish and Wildlife Service, "National Wildlife Refuge System Overview," fact sheet, April 2013.

[158] U.S. Fish and Wildlife Service, 2009, pp. 1-2.

- Provide a clear statement of direction for the future management of the refuges;
- Provide long-term continuity in management;
- Communicate the Service's management priorities for the refuges to its conservation partners, neighbors, visitors, and the general public;
- Provide an opportunity for the public to help shape the future management of the refuges;
- Ensure that management programs on the refuges are consistent with the mandates of the NWRS and the purposes for which each refuge was established;
- Ensure that the management of the refuges fully considers resource priorities and management strategies identified in other federal, state, and local plans;
- Provide a basis for budget requests to support the refuge's needs, staffing, operations, maintenance, and capital improvements; and
- Evaluate existing and proposed uses of each refuge to ensure that they are compatible with the refuge purpose(s) as well as the maintenance of biological integrity, diversity, and environmental health.[159]

Therefore, the CCP is the key guidance and management document for an NWR. The last CCP for the DNWR Complex was developed in 2009 and we use it as a key source of information for the DNWR, including understanding the wilderness status of the DNWR. When this CCP was developed, an EIS also was developed for it because of the requirements of the NEPA process. It is USFWS policy to combine the CCP with its EIS into one document which was done for the DNWR Complex CCP in 2009.

It is important to note that a NWR's mission is very different from the mission of BLM. BLM lands are managed for multiple purposes and allow more impact on wildlife and their habitat than NWR lands. An NWR is managed for wildlife conservation and wildlife-dependent recreation. As outlined in the National Wildlife Refuge System Improvement Act of 1997, six areas of wildlife-dependent recreation considered appropriate on refuges: hunting, fishing, wildlife observation, photography and environmental education and interpretation. An NWR has more restrictions on activities than does BLM land, which means that even if the NTTR portion of the DNWR was not wilderness, USAF operations would face more restrictions on its operations there than on portions of the NTTR that are withdrawn from BLM lands.

The Desert National Wildlife Refuge

The Desert National Wildlife Refuge (DNWR) is located in southern Nevada. It was originally established as a Desert Game Range by Executive Order 7373 in 1936 to provide habitat and protection for desert bighorn sheep. The original size was 2.25 million acres. It is now called the Desert National Wildlife Refuge or the Desert National Wildlife Range.

---

[159] U.S. Fish and Wildlife Service, 2009, pp. 1-2.

DNWR currently contains 1.6 million acres (643,000 hectares) and is the largest wildlife refuge outside of Alaska. The refuge transitions from the Mojave to the Great Basin Desert and contains more than 500 plant species and 320 bird species.[160]

DNWR is managed as part of the Desert National Wildlife Refuge Complex. The Complex consists of four refuges located in southern Nevada: Ash Meadows, Desert, Moapa Valley, and Pahranagat National Wildlife Refuges.

> A National Wildlife Refuge Complex is an administrative grouping of two or more refuges, wildlife management areas or other refuge conservation areas that are primarily managed from a central office location. Refuges are grouped into a complex structure because they occur in a similar ecological region, such as a watershed or specific habitat type, and have a related purpose and management needs. Typically, a project leader or complex manager oversees the general management of all refuges within the complex and refuge managers are responsible for operations at specific refuges. Supporting staff, composed of administrative, law enforcement, refuge manager, biological, fire, visitor services, and maintenance professionals, are centrally located and support all refuges within the complex.[161]

USFWS developed five goals for the management of the DNWR as outlined in the 2009 DNWR Complex CCP:

> **Bighorn Sheep (Goal 1).** Maintain and, where necessary, restore healthy population levels of bighorn sheep on Desert NWR within each of the six major mountain ranges.
>
> **Wildlife Diversity (Goal 2).** Maintain the existing natural diversity of native wildlife and plants, including special-status species, at Desert NWR.
>
> **Specially designated Areas (Goal 3).** Manage specially designated areas such that they augment the purposes of the Desert NWR.
>
> **Visitor Services (Goal 4).** Provide visitors with opportunities to understand, appreciate, and enjoy the fragile Mojave/Great Basin Desert ecosystem.
>
> **Cultural Resources (Goal 5).** Manage cultural resources for their educational, scientific, and traditional cultural values for the benefit of present and future generations of refuge users, communities, and culturally affiliated tribes.[162]

USFWS staff used these goals to identify specific objectives and strategies and develop alternatives with specific management actions.[163]

---

[160] U.S. Fish and Wildlife Service, "Desert National Wildlife Range: About the Refuge," last updated July 22, 2013.

[161] U.S. Fish and Wildlife Service, 2013.

[162] U.S. Fish and Wildlife Service, 2009, p. 1-32.

[163] U.S. Fish and Wildlife Service, 2009, p. 1-32.

NTTR Portion of the DNWR

Most of the NTTR South Range overlaps the western portion of the DNWR, and over time, the amount of overlap noted in official documents has changed. Some of the differences may be the result of updated surveys using more accurate measurement technologies. Others could be caused by differences in what land is counted because of changes in who has primary management responsibilities for some areas in the range. For completeness, we note the different values we have found as the area of the NTTR South Range that overlaps with the DNWR:

- 1971: 819,000 acres[164]
- 1997: 845,787 acres[165]
- 2009: 816,400 acres[166]
- 2010: 826,000 acres[167]
- 2013: 842,254 acres[168]

What is more important than these relatively minor variations in estimates of the amount of overlap is the wilderness status of DNWR lands that are in the NTTR.

What is the Wilderness Status of NTTR Lands within the DNWR?

Before discussing the wilderness status of NTTR lands, it is important to understand the different classifications of potential wilderness lands on federal lands. Three different designations are used to refer to wilderness: "recommended wilderness," "proposed wilderness" and "wilderness study area." In some cases, BLM, NPS, USFWS and USFS use these terms differently. For instance, "recommended wilderness" has different meanings for the Forest Service compared to the Fish and Wildlife Service. Since we are concerned with the DNWR we present the official USFWS definitions here:

> **"Wilderness Study Area (WSA).** An area we are considering for wilderness designation. We identify and establish WSAs through the inventory component of a wilderness review. WSAs include all areas that are still undergoing the review process, areas for which a final determination of suitability and recommendation for wilderness designation in the record of decision for the comprehensive conservation plan (CCP) is pending, and areas recommended for

---

164 See *Desert Wilderness Proposal: Desert National Wildlife Range*, 1971. This document was the basis for the 1974 wilderness proposal submitted to Congress. A copy of the document can be found in Appendix I of the August 2009 *Final Comprehensive Conservation Plan and Environmental Impact Statement* for the Desert National Wildlife Refuge Complex.

165 U.S. Department of the Air Force and U.S. Department of the Interior, 1997.

166 Nellis Air Force Base, 2009. However, page 56 of this document also says that 848,000 acres are co-withdrawn and that 890,000 acres are co-managed.

167 Nellis Air Force Base, 2010.

168 U.S. Department of the Air Force and U.S. Fish and Wildlife Service, 2013.

> wilderness designation in a final CCP and awaiting approval by the Director. We consider areas recommended by the Director "recommended wilderness."[169]
>
> "**Recommended Wilderness**. An area of the Refuge System that the Director of the Service has recommended to the Secretary through the Assistant Secretary for Fish, Wildlife, and Parks for inclusion in the NWPS."[170]
>
> "**Proposed Wilderness**. An area of the Refuge System that the Secretary of the Interior (Secretary) has recommended to the President for inclusion in the NWPS. The President then transmits the wilderness proposal to Congress. Once the Secretary transmits the recommendation to the President, we consider the area "proposed wilderness" and will manage it as designated wilderness."[171]

As was discussed earlier, because of the Wilderness Act of 1964, USFWS had to review all of its national wildlife refuge lands, including the DNWR, for their suitability for wilderness preservation. The secretary of the Interior then made wilderness proposals to the President and Congress. In the early 1970s, a proposal was made to designate approximately 1.4 million acres within the Desert NWR as wilderness. Though this wilderness proposal was submitted to Congress in 1974, it never has been acted upon.[172] The NTTR portion of the DNWR was part of this proposal and it still is considered "proposed wilderness" according to USFWS, as stated in the DNWR Complex CCP of 2009.

With this original proposal, a presidential recommendation was made that Congress defer action until a mineral survey was completed. A mineral assessment for the DNWR was "completed in 1993 as part of the mineral withdrawal, which was later completed in 1999."[173] A final EIS for the DNWR wilderness proposal was completed in 1975. Since Congress has yet to act on this proposed wilderness area within the DNWR, the area continues to be managed to protect its wilderness values.[174]

In the original wilderness study of the DNWR which became the "1971 Desert NWR Wilderness Proposal" sent to Congress in 1974, the wilderness study area included all of the DNWR and 58,000 acres of adjacent public lands that were considered logical extensions of the DNWR. This area was divided into 12 study areas because of wildlife management and development programs and plans, Air Force use, and private in-holdings, or privately owned land within the boundaries of public lands (see Figure C.1). Permanent road and vehicle trails, contour lines, and legal subdivisions served as unit boundaries. About 88 percent of this wilderness study area, or 1,443,100 acres, in the first seven units (see map in Figure C.1) was

---

[169] U.S. Fish and Wildlife Service, *USFWS Service Manual*, Part 610 FW 1, November 7, 2008, pp. 4-5.

[170] U.S. Fish and Wildlife Service, *USFWS Service Manual,* 2008, p. 3.

[171] U.S. Fish and Wildlife Service, *USFWS Service Manual,* 2008, p. 3.

[172] U.S. Fish and Wildlife Service, 2009, Appendix I.

[173] U.S. Fish and Wildlife Service, 2009, pp. 1-28 and 1-29.

[174] U.S. Fish and Wildlife Service, 2009, p. 1-29.

judged as suitable for wilderness.[175] These seven units, varying in size from 40,900 acres to 440,000 acres, became the wilderness proposal. Unit X was excluded from consideration because it included

> lands used for target areas by the Air Force as provided by the agreement which authorizes their use. The areas subject to physical disturbances are located in valleys below 3,600 feet elevation and were so delineated, as contour lines provide the only practical basis for establishing a wilderness management boundary in the absence of a legal land survey.[176]

Units XI and XII, which are located along the north boundary of the DNWR, also were excluded. They are within the Air Force bombing and gunnery range and contain target facilities where "much physical disturbance has occurred in conjunction with these activities." Other excluded areas included unit IX, because of private in-holdings and unit VIII because of Corn Creek administrative subheadquarters and eight private inholdings (see map again).[177]

There also were some proposed stipulations:

- Permanent roads and primitive vehicle trails which serve as wilderness unit boundaries shall be 16 feet in width, with a total right-of-way 116 feet in width, measuring 58 feet on either side of the center line of the existing road or trail. This will provide a suitable area for roadside parking and a buffer for future road maintenance.
- The primitive terminal access vehicle trails excluded from the proposed wilderness shall be 10 feet in width, with a total right-of-way 110 feet, measuring 58 feet on either side of the center line of the existing trails. The vehicle parking and turn-around area at the end of these trails shall be an area two acres in size.
- Use of vehicles on Nye Canyon, White Sage Gap, Pine Spring, Mormon Well Spring, Wamp Spring and Quail Spring Trails will be authorized for administrative purposes only.
- Surface exploration for minerals within the proposed wilderness units would not be permitted.
- Use of the Warm Spring sheep trap will be authorized for trapping and transplanting of desert bighorns.[178]

---

[175] See a copy of the original 1971 proposal in U.S. Fish and Wildlife Service, 2009, Appendix I-2.

[176] U.S. Fish and Wildlife Service, 2009, Appendix I-2.

[177] U.S. Fish and Wildlife Service, 2009, Appendix I-2.

[178] U.S. Fish and Wildlife Service, 2009, Appendix I-2.

Figure C.1. Wilderness Units in the Original Desert Wilderness Proposal for the DNWR

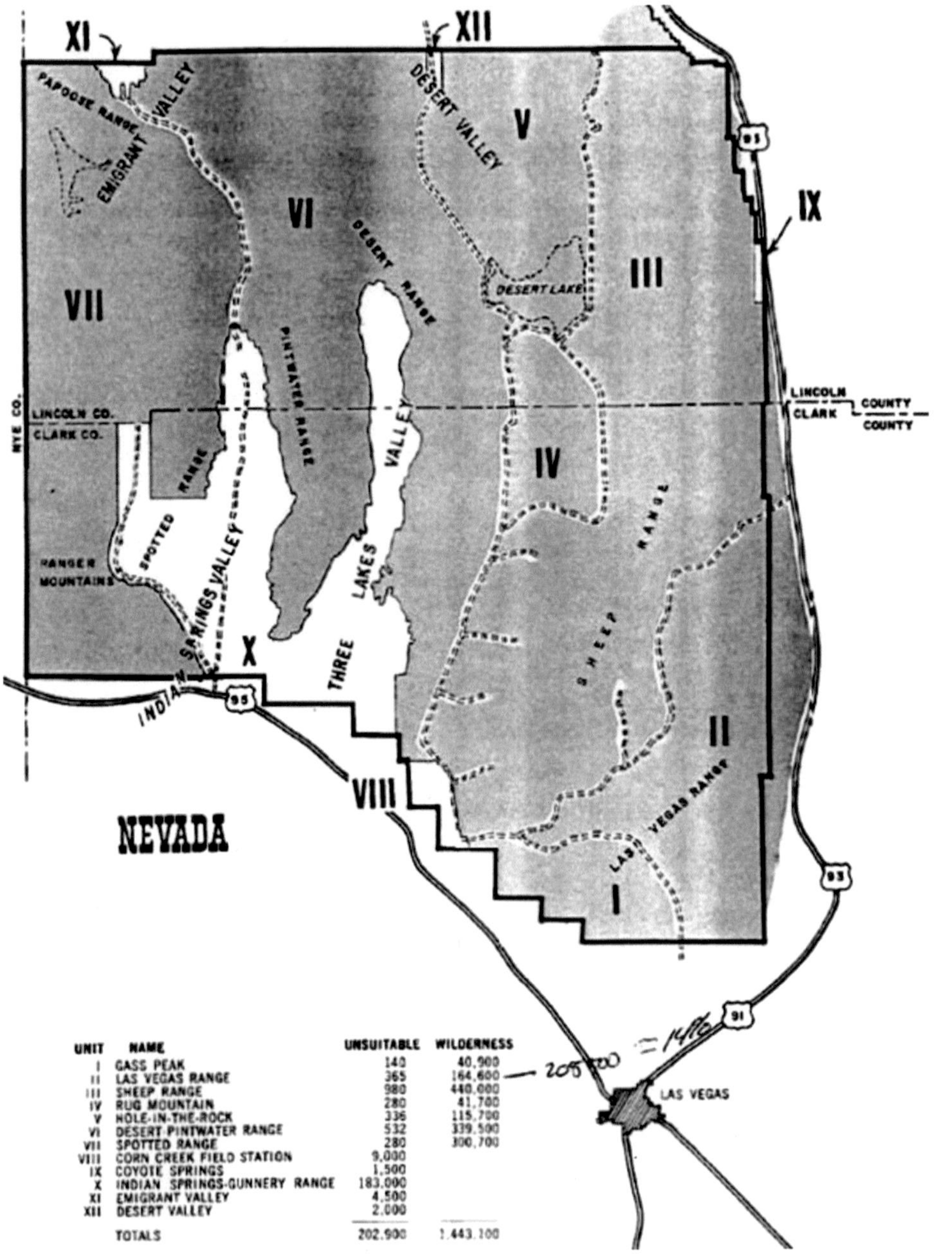

UNIT	NAME	UNSUITABLE	WILDERNESS
I	GASS PEAK	140	40,900
II	LAS VEGAS RANGE	365	164,600
III	SHEEP RANGE	980	440,000
IV	RUG MOUNTAIN	280	41,700
V	HOLE-IN-THE-ROCK	336	115,700
VI	DESERT-PINTWATER RANGE	532	339,500
VII	SPOTTED RANGE	280	300,700
VIII	CORN CREEK FIELD STATION	9,000	
IX	COYOTE SPRINGS	1,500	
X	INDIAN SPRINGS-GUNNERY RANGE	183,000	
XI	EMIGRANT VALLEY	4,500	
XII	DESERT VALLEY	2,000	
	TOTALS	202,900	1,443,100

SOURCE: U.S. Fish and Wildlife Service, 2009, Appendix I-2, 1971 Desert NWR Wilderness Proposal.

However, this wilderness review and proposal was made 40 years ago. The wilderness character of some of these lands may have changed since then. The DNWR Complex CCP of 2009 recognized this and stated that it was going to submit a revised proposal regarding the DNWR proposed wilderness area:

> As part of the CCP implementation, the Service plans to prepare a revised proposal which includes technical corrections to the existing proposed wilderness such as: correcting overlap with US Air Force's bombing range; allowing

> repair/relocation of hazardous sections of roads; and allowing the use of helicopters to repair/maintain water developments and access remote areas for wildlife surveys. Details of these revisions will be provided in a revised proposal.[179]

It sounds as if USFWS was planning to conduct an analysis to update this proposal It appears that USFWS should be conducting a wilderness review. "A wilderness review is the process we [USFWS staff] follow to identify and recommend for congressional designation Refuge System lands and waters that merit inclusion in the National Wilderness Preservation System (NWPS). Wilderness reviews are a required element of comprehensive conservation plans (CCP)." "This process includes interagency and tribal coordination, public involvement, and National Environmental Policy Act (NEPA) compliance." Wilderness reviews are conducted as part of a scheduled CCP or CCP revision, and at a minimum are done at every 15 years through the CCP process. USFWS says it may conduct a wilderness review as part of a CCP revision "any time that significant new information becomes available, ecological conditions change, major refuge expansion occurs, or when we identify the need to do so during plan review."[180] It seems like the status of this land may have changed enough during the last 40 years to warrant such a wilderness review. However, given the time and expense of the wilderness review process (described in Appendix D), it is unlikely that the USFWS is conducting a formal wilderness review process, especially since the logical time to do that was during the DNWR Complex CCP update in 2009.

Management of Wilderness on National Wildlife Refuges

The proposed wilderness areas on the DNWR must be managed as wilderness, so USFWS must follow the wilderness procedures for NWRs. NWR staff must administer wilderness areas, proposed wilderness, recommended wilderness, and WSAs in accordance with approved CCPs and wilderness stewardship plans (WSPs). If an NWR has an approved CCP that sufficiently addresses the wilderness areas it may not have an approved WSP. A WSP guides the preservation, stewardship, and uses of particular wilderness areas:

> The WSP is a step-down management plan. ... The WSP provides detailed strategies and implementation schedules for meeting the broader wilderness goals and objectives identified in the refuge comprehensive conservation plan (CCP). We [NWR staff] develop WSPs using the planning process guidance in 602 FW 1, 3, and 4.[181]

---

[179] U.S. Fish and Wildlife Service, 2009, Appendix I.

[180] U.S. Fish and Wildlife Service, *USFWS Service Manual*, 610 FW 4, November 7, 2008, p. 44.

[181] U.S. Fish and Wildlife Service, *USFWS Service Manual*, 610 FW 3, November 7, 2008, p. 38.

The USFWS says that a WSP contains "specific and measurable stewardship strategies and implementation schedules that address the preservation or, as appropriate, restoration of cultural and natural resource values and conditions." A WSP, it says, must describe the strategies and actions USFWS will use to preserve the wilderness resource and the link between "those strategies and actions and the wilderness goals and objectives identified in the CCP." The WSP also includes "indicators, standards, conditions, or thresholds that define adverse impacts on wilderness character and values and that will trigger stewardship actions to reduce or prevent those impacts."[182]

The USFWS Wilderness Stewardship Policy (610 FW) provides the guidance for how to manage wilderness and proposed wilderness on NWR lands. This guidance describes what wilderness is; how to evaluate wilderness status; NWR staff roles in protecting and managing wilderness; and what activities are allowed and prohibited in wilderness. This policy also provides an overview of the process for allowing some limited prohibited activities in wilderness for management purposes. This process is called a minimum requirement analysis (MRA):

> A decision-making process, documented in writing, that we [USFWS staff] use to determine if proposed refuge management activities conducted in wilderness are necessary to administer the area as wilderness and to accomplish the purposes of the refuge, including Wilderness Act purposes. If the activities are necessary, the MRA also describes how to minimize resultant impacts.[183]

USFWS staff conduct a MRA "for all proposed refuge management activities that involve a generally prohibited use." [184]

> If the refuge has an approved WSP less than 15 years old and it includes a written MRA for each proposed refuge management activity, we [USFWS] may carry out those activities as described in the plan. The analysis in the WSP must include an estimate of how frequently each activity will take place and the intensity of the activity. If circumstances significantly change or we want to allow the same activity in a significantly different part of the wilderness, we must prepare another MRA.[185]

Since NWR-proposed and officially designated wilderness areas must be managed to preserve the character of wilderness, understanding what that character is is important to understanding NWR wilderness management. The USFWS Wilderness Stewardship Policy also defines wilderness character:

> Preserving "wilderness character," referenced throughout the Wilderness Act and this policy, is a primary criterion for judging the appropriateness of proposed

---

[182] U.S. Fish and Wildlife Service, *USFWS Service Manual*, 610 FW 3, p. 38.

[183] U.S. Fish and Wildlife Service, *USFWS Service Manual*, 610 FW 3, p. 3.

[184] U.S. Fish and Wildlife Service, *USFWS Service Manual*, 610 FW 3, p. 11.

[185] U.S. Fish and Wildlife Service, *USFWS Service Manual*, 610 FW 1, p. 12.

refuge management activities and refuge uses, including public use and enjoyment, in wilderness. Preserving wilderness character requires that we maintain both the tangible and intangible aspects of wilderness. Wilderness character increases as it approaches the highest measure of natural conditions and being untrammeled.

"The tangible and intangible aspects of wilderness include:

(1) Maintaining the natural, scenic condition of the land;

(2) Providing environments for native plants and animals, including those threatened or endangered;

(3) Maintaining watersheds and airsheds in a healthy condition;

(4) Maintaining natural night skies and soundscapes;

(5) Retaining the primeval character of and influence on the land;

(6) Serving as a benchmark for ecological studies; and

(7) Providing opportunities for solitude, primitive and unconfined outdoor recreation, risk, adventure, education, personal growth experiences, a sense of connection with nature and values beyond one's self, a link to our American cultural heritage, and mental and spiritual restoration in the absence of urban pressures."[186]

---

[186] U.S. Fish and Wildlife Service, *USFWS Service Manual*, 610 FW 1, p. 9.

Appendix D. Process for Determining What NWR Lands Should Be Wilderness

In this appendix, we describe the process that USFWS currently uses to determine whether NWR lands should be proposed for wilderness. This process is called the wilderness review process. As outlined in the USFWS Wilderness Stewardship Policy (610 FW), USFWS has a range of specific analysis, public involvement, and documentation steps that they are required to take before proposing NWR lands as possible wilderness. This process is time-consuming and expensive.

The Wilderness Review Process

As was briefly mentioned in the main report, a wilderness review is the process the USFWS follows to identify and recommend for congressional designation NWR lands that merit inclusion in the National Wilderness Preservation System. The wilderness review process consists of three phases:

- **Inventory**. USFWS staff identifies "land and waters that meet the minimum criteria for wilderness." They call these areas wilderness study areas (WSAs).
- **Wilderness Study.** USFWS staff evaluate WSAs "to determine if they are suitable for wilderness designation."
- **Recommendation.** USFWS staff use the findings of this study to determine if they "will recommend the area for designation as wilderness in the final CCP." They report their "wilderness recommendations from the Director through the Secretary of the Interior (Secretary) and the President to Congress in a wilderness study report."[187]

The Inventory Analysis of Minimum Wilderness Criteria

For the inventory phase, the USFWS uses the following criteria to evaluate NWR areas as potential wilderness:

1. Size
2. Naturalness
3. Opportunities for solitude or primitive recreation
4. Supplemental values[188]

[187] U.S. Fish and Wildlife Service, *USFWS Service Manual*, 610 FW 4, p. 44.

[188] U.S. Fish and Wildlife Service, *USFWS Service Manual*, 610 FW 4, p. 45.

If an NWR land area meets these criteria, then it is considered a WSA. Here we summarize the process of applying these criteria to determine if the lands meet these basic wilderness criteria. This discussion follows the wilderness review process outlined in the USFWS Wilderness Stewardship Policy, (610 FW) which provides the guidance for how to conduct a wilderness review for NWR lands.

Size Evaluation

An area meets the wilderness criteria if the area:

- Has no permanent roads and is 5,000 contiguous acres or more
- Is a roadless island
- Has no permanent roads and is of sufficient size to make its preservation and use in an unimpaired condition practicable
- Is an area with no permanent roads and less than 5,000 contiguous acres that is contiguous with other federal lands that are a designated wilderness, a WSA, a proposed wilderness, or a recommended wilderness area.[189]

Naturalness Evaluation

The second criterion for a wilderness area regards naturalness and whether the area generally appears to be natural and has a relatively unnoticeable human presence. This criterion is subjective. Specific criteria as outlined in USFWS wilderness review guidance discuss the ambiguities of this evaluation and the fact that it recognizes that some human presence is acceptable. We present these criteria and bold sections that are most relevant for the NTTR DNWR areas:

> A. We make a distinction between an area's "apparent naturalness" and "historic conditions" in the context of biological integrity, diversity, and environmental health. The term "historic conditions" refers to the condition of the landscape in a particular area before the onset of significant, human-caused change. The term "apparent naturalness" refers to **whether or not an area looks natural to the average visitor who is not familiar with historic conditions versus human-affected ecosystems in a given area**. We address the question of the presence or absence of apparent naturalness (i.e., are the works of humans substantially unnoticeable to the average visitor?) in the inventory phase of the wilderness review. In the study phase of the wilderness review, we make an assessment of an area's existing levels of biological integrity, diversity, and environmental health.
>
> B. We avoid an approach to assessing naturalness that limits wilderness designation only to those areas judged pristine.
>
> C. We use caution in assessing the effects on naturalness that relatively minor human impacts create. **An area being evaluated may include some human impacts provided they are substantially unnoticeable in the unit as a whole.**

---

[189] U.S. Fish and Wildlife Service, *USFWS Service Manual*, 610 FW 4, p. 45.

> Examples of manmade features that would not disqualify an area for consideration as a WSA include: trails, trail signs, bridges, fire towers, fire breaks, fire presuppression facilities, pit toilets, fisheries enhancement facilities (such as fish traps and stream barriers), fire rings, hitching posts, snow gauges, water quantity and quality measuring devices, research monitoring markers and devices, wildlife enhancement facilities, radio repeater sites, air quality monitoring devices, fencing, spring developments, and small reservoirs. **Even with these features, an area may express wilderness character and values.**
>
> D. **We may disqualify portions of an area from consideration where significant human-caused hazards make that area unsafe for public use, such as contaminated sites or the existence of unexploded ordnance from military activity.** Once these conditions are corrected, we may then consider that portion of the area.
>
> E. **We do not disqualify areas from further wilderness study solely on the basis of the "sights and sounds" of civilization located outside the areas.** Where human impacts are outside the area being inventoried, we do not normally consider them in assessing naturalness. However, if an **outside impact of major significance exists, we should note it and evaluate it** in the inventory conclusions. **Human impacts outside the area should not automatically lead us to conclude that an area lacks wilderness characteristics.**
>
> F. **We do not disqualify areas from further wilderness study solely on the basis of established or proposed refuge management activities or refuge uses that require the use of temporary roads, motor vehicles, motorized equipment, motorboats, mechanical transport, landing of aircraft, structures,** and installations generally prohibited in designated wilderness (see definition of "generally prohibited use" in 610 FW 1.5). The physical impacts of these practices should be the focus of the naturalness evaluation. We evaluate existing and proposed refuge management activities and refuge uses in the study phase of the wilderness review.[190]

Applying these criteria to NWR lands means that most areas being proposed as wilderness would look "natural to the average visitor who is not familiar with historic conditions versus human-affected ecosystems in a given area." In addition, most of the areas should be considered natural, untrammeled, and undeveloped (with an absence of permanent structures, such as roads and buildings) which are the three cornerstones of the wilderness character.[191]

It is important to note that just because an area has military activities and unexploded ordnance (UXO), it is not automatically excluded from being considered suitable for wilderness. In fact, there are other NWRs with military activities and UXO, such as Nomans Land Island NWR, where the property passed this naturalness criteria and was considered suitable as wilderness. Nomans Land Island is a 640-acre island off the coast of Martha's Vineyard in Massachusetts which the Navy used for aerial gunnery from 1942 to 1996. The land was

---

[190] U.S. Fish and Wildlife Service, *USFWS Service Manual*, 610 FW 4, p. 46.

[191] U.S Fish and Wildlife Service, "Rose Atoll National Wildlife Refuge Draft Comprehensive Conservation Plan and Environmental Assessment," undated, p. E-4.

transferred to DOI to become a NWR in the late 1990s as a sanctuary for migratory birds. It is now an NWR within a military reservation boundary and the Navy still uses the island for minimal non-training purposes, such as having three storage structures there. Because it was a former gunnery range there is still UXO on the island and it is closed to the public. In fact, on its website, the Nomans Land Island NWR has posted the following warning: "Due to the potential safety risks associated with unexploded ordnance, the refuge is closed to all public uses."[192] Because there is no public access, the UXO issue did not stop the area from being found suitable as wilderness during the wilderness review process and being recommended as wilderness. In fact the final CCP for Nomans Land Island NWR states:

> The presence of UXO may disqualify an area from wilderness consideration where " … human-caused hazards make that area unsafe for public use, such as contaminated sites or the existence of unexploded ordnance" … [H]owever, public access has not been allowed on the island since the Navy began their operations, and the Refuge will continue to enforce the ban on public access in the future.[193]

In some ways, having UXO actually helps the NWR mission by ensuring no public access to the island, making it better for migratory birds. As a Boston newspaper article stated, "But this nightmare for human visitors [dangerous UXO] is a blessing for its avian guests. Due to its undisturbed nature and shortage of predators, Nomans Land is an important stop on the Atlantic Flyway for songbirds migrating south as far as South America."[194]

Evaluation of Opportunities for Solitude or Primitive Recreation

The third criterion for a wilderness area has to do with opportunities for solitude or primitive recreation. As specified in the USFWS wilderness review guidance:

> How does the Service evaluate outstanding opportunities for solitude or a primitive and unconfined type of recreation during inventory? Section 2(c) of the Wilderness Act defines wilderness as an area that has outstanding opportunities for solitude or a primitive and unconfined type of recreation. An area does not need to have outstanding opportunities for both elements and does not need to have outstanding opportunities on every acre.[195]

Each area is assessed "on its own merits to determine if an outstanding opportunity exists," without comparing areas. In addition, "An area does not have to be open to public entry and use.

---

[192] U.S. Fish and Wildlife Service, "Nomans Land Island NWR," February 24, 2014.

[193] U.S. Fish and Wildlife Service, *Nomans Island National Wildlife Refuge Final Comprehensive Conservation Plan*, September 2010, p. C-5.

[194] Brian MacQuarrie, "Officials want it to stay Nomans Land," *Boston Globe*, July 12, 2010.

[195] U.S. Fish and Wildlife Service, *USFWS Service Manual*, 610 FW 4, p. 47.

Congress has designated several Service wilderness areas that are closed to public use to conserve wildlife and fragile habitats."[196]

The key questions asked are: Does the area offer the opportunity for primitive and unconfined recreational activities like camping, hiking, and hunting? Does the area provide opportunities for solitude? How significant are these opportunities? Since wilderness areas can be closed to the public to help conserve wildlife and habitats, does the proposed NWR area, like the NTTR DNWR wilderness area, play a role in conserving wildlife and habitats? Is the conservation of such wildlife and their habitats considered significant enough?

Evaluation of Supplemental Values

"Supplemental values" refers to whether the area contains any ecological, geological, or other features of scientific, educational, scenic, or historic value. A wilderness area does not need to have these values, but they should be documented if they are present. For example, the NTTR portions of the DNWR that are proposed wilderness include areas of ecological value, most notably areas that help protect habitat for the desert bighorn sheep, desert tortoise, and golden eagles.

The Wilderness Study

The second phase of a wilderness review is when USFWS staff conduct a wilderness study of NWR areas that met the wilderness criteria and are considered WSAs. As outlined in USFWS wilderness review guidance:

> We [USFWS staff] study each WSA identified in the inventory to analyze all values (e.g., ecological, recreational, cultural, economic, symbolic), resources (e.g., wildlife, water, vegetation, minerals, soils), public uses, and refuge management activities within the area. The analysis includes an evaluation of whether we can effectively manage the WSA to preserve its wilderness character. We analyze these elements through the refuge planning process to determine the most appropriate management direction for each WSA.[197]

USFWS staff then evaluate an "All Wilderness Alternative" and a "No Wilderness Alternative" for each of the identified WSAs "to compare the benefits and impacts of managing the area as wilderness as opposed to managing the area under an alternate set of goals, objectives, and strategies that do not involve wilderness designation." They also may develop and evaluate the benefits and impacts of "Partial Wilderness Alternatives" that are used to consider managing part of the WSA as wilderness. Such partial alternatives are developed to "minimize resource conflicts or improve the capability of managing an area as wilderness."[198]

---

[196] U.S. Fish and Wildlife Service, *USFWS Service Manual*, 610 FW 4, p. 47.

[197] U.S. Fish and Wildlife Service, *USFWS Service Manual*, 610 FW 4, p. 47.

[198] U.S. Fish and Wildlife Service, *USFWS Service Manual*, 610 FW 4, p. 47.

For each of these management alternatives, USFWS conducts an environmental analysis that addresses benefits and impacts to wilderness values and other resources under each management alternative.

In this wilderness study, USFWS staff evaluates how each alternative will:

> Achieve the purposes of the Wilderness Act and the NWPS
> - Affect achieving refuge or planning unit purpose(s);
> - Affect that refuge's contribution toward achieving the Refuge System mission;
> - Affect maintaining and, where appropriate, restoring biological integrity, diversity, and environmental health at various landscape scales; and
> - Meet other legal and policy mandates.[199]

In this wilderness study, USFWS staff also assess "the area's suitability for management and preservation as wilderness with regard to the area's primary purposes as a refuge. The information, analysis, and decisions in the CCP and associated NEPA document provide the rationale for wilderness suitability determinations and the basic source of information throughout the public, executive, and legislative review processes that follow."[200]

USFWS staff evaluate whether a WSA can be effectively managed as wilderness:

> Being able to manage an area as wilderness is one of the criteria we [USFWS] evaluate and consider in the wilderness study phase to determine whether all or part of a WSA is suitable for wilderness designation. We [USFWS] must be reasonably certain that we can manage an area recommended as suitable for wilderness designation over the long term to maintain the wilderness character while accomplishing refuge purposes and the Refuge System mission. We [USFWS] evaluate the potential for adjusting a WSA's boundary to improve wilderness manageability and analyze feasible boundary adjustments in a "Partial Wilderness Alternative."[201]

To determine if they can manage an area, USFWS staff consider how the following types of factors would individually and collectively affect their overall ability to manage an area as wilderness:

> A. Existing Private Rights. We [USFWS] describe the type, extent, and validity of private rights in the WSA. How would the exercise of property rights owned by a party other than the Federal Government, such as privately owned subsurface rights, limit our ability to maintain an area's wilderness values and character?
>
> B. Land Status and Service Jurisdiction. We [USFWS] document the land status and extent of Service jurisdiction for lands and waters within and adjacent to the WSA. We [USFWS] ask:

---

[199] U.S. Fish and Wildlife Service, *USFWS Service Manual*, 610 FW 4, p. 47.

[200] U.S. Fish and Wildlife Service, *USFWS Service Manual*, 610 FW 4, pp. 47-48.

[201] U.S. Fish and Wildlife Service, *USFWS Service Manual*, 610 FW 4, p. 48.

> (1) Does the Service have adequate jurisdiction over the lands and waters to ensure maintenance of wilderness resources and character within the WSA?
>
> (2) What is the extent of non-Federal lands within the WSA, and what are the prospects for acquisition?
>
> (3) How would the overall land ownership pattern affect our ability to manage the area as wilderness (e.g., private access to inholdings)?
>
> C. Refuge Management Activities and Refuge Uses. We [USFWS] document and evaluate existing and planned refuge management activities and refuge uses in the WSAs. We [USFWS] ask:
>
> (1) Do these activities currently involve or require use of generally prohibited uses?
>
> (2) How would continuation or implementation of these activities and uses affect our ability to manage the area as wilderness?
>
> (3) Can we modify or eliminate these activities or uses to improve our ability to manage the area as wilderness while still accomplishing refuge purposes?[202]

The Recommendation Phase

If the wilderness study conclusions include a preferred alternative that includes some areas that USFWS thinks should be recommended for wilderness, then the final CCP identifies the WSAs that USFWS staff has determined are suitable for recommendation as wilderness. It also outlines specific management directions to maintain the areas' wilderness character. USFWS staff "manage those areas in accordance with the CCP until Congress makes a decision on the areas or until we [USFWS] amend the CCP to modify or remove the suitable wilderness determination."[203] In addition, for areas determined suitable for wilderness designation, the final CCP is required to state:

> The [name areas] wilderness study areas have been determined to be suitable for wilderness designation. These recommendations are preliminary administrative determinations that will receive further review and possible modification by the Director of the U.S. Fish and Wildlife Service, the Secretary, and/or the President of the United States. Congress has reserved the authority to make final decisions on wilderness designation.[204]

NEPA and the Council on Environmental Quality require that USFWS conduct a legislative EIS for a proposed wilderness area.

When submitting a wilderness proposal to the president and Congress, USFWS includes with the wilderness proposal the legislative EIS, a wilderness study report, and other required documentation and information. In most cases, USFWS will have prepared an EIS for a CCP that

---

[202] U.S. Fish and Wildlife Service, *USFWS Service Manual*, 610 FW 4, p. 48.

[203] U.S. Fish and Wildlife Service, *USFWS Service Manual*, 610 FW 4, p. 48.

[204] U.S. Fish and Wildlife Service, *USFWS Service Manual*, 610 FW 4, p. 49.

includes recommendations for wilderness designation. USFWS may include wilderness recommendations in a final CCP in which an environmental assessment has been prepared. In these cases, USFWS subsequently will prepare a legislative EIS for those WSAs, drawing from the information and analyses prepared for the CCP.

The wilderness study report is a summary of the wilderness review and includes the following information:

- The Director's wilderness recommendation and rationale.
- A general description of and background history for each area studied.
- An analysis of each area's values, resources, and uses.
- Evidence that we [USFWS] notified the public about the proposal, including publication in the Federal Register and notice(s) in local newspapers.
- Evidence that we [USFWS] notified the Governor and other concerned officials (e.g., State, other Federal, local, and tribal) at least 30 days before holding a public hearing(s).
- A summary and analysis of comments received and the public hearing record.
- Evidence of direct notification and request for comments from the State Historic Preservation Officer about the presence or absence of significant cultural resources.
- A legal description and map showing the recommended wilderness boundary.
- A CCP and a legislative EIS.[205]

If the final determination in a CCP is that a NWR WSA is not suitable for wilderness designation, then USFWS staff document the decision in the CCP and end the study process. These NWR areas that were determined unsuitable for wilderness designation are managed following the management direction outlined in the CCP.

[205] U.S. Fish and Wildlife Service, *USFWS Service Manual*, 610 FW 4, p. 50.

Bibliography

Abbey, Edward, *Desert Solitaire*, New York: Ballantine Books, 1968.

Birdandhike.com, "Cow Camp Road," 2012. As of August 31, 2015: http://www.birdandhike.com/Hike/DNWR/Roads_DNWR/Road_CowCamp/_CowCamp_Rd.htm

———, "La Madre Mountains Wilderness Area," 2013. As of August 31, 2015: http://www.birdandhike.com/Wilderness/LaMadre/_LaMadre.htm

———, "Muddy Mountains Wilderness Area," 2011. As of August 31, 2015: http://www.birdandhike.com/Wilderness/MuddyMts/_Muddy.htm

Cordell, H. Ken, John C. Bergstrom, and J. M. Bowker, *The Multiple Values of Wilderness*, State College, Pa.: Venture Publishing, Inc., 2005.

———, Carter J. Betz, Becky Stephens, Shela Mou, and Gary T. Green, *How Do Americans View Wilderness?* U.S. Forest Service, Internet Research Information Series, January 2008. As of August 31, 2015: http://warnell.forestry.uga.edu/nrrt/nsre/IRISWild/IrisWild1rpt.pdf

Daniel Boone National Forest, "Red River Gorge Geological Area," undated. As of August 31, 2015: http://www.fs.usda.gov/recarea/dbnf/recreation/recarea/?recid=39458

Dungan, Ron, "Project Near Ajo Gives Pronghorns Second Chance," *Arizona Republic*, February 6, 2010, As of August 31, 2015: http://www.azcentral.com/news/articles/2010/02/06/20100206pronghorn.html

Fort Bragg Morale, Welfare and Recreation Program, "Warrior Adventure Quest," 2011. As of August 31, 2015: http://www.fortbraggmwr.com/recreation/warrior-adventure-quest/

Johnson, Jerry D., and Raymond Rasker, The Role of Economic and Quality of Life Values in Rural Business Location," *Journal of Rural Studies*, Vol. 11, No. 4, 1995. As of August 31, 2015: http://www.sciencedirect.com/science/article/pii/0743016795000291

Lachman, Beth E., Anny Wong and Susan A. Resetar, *The Thin Green Line: An Assessment of DoD's Readiness and Environmental Protection Initiative to Buffer Installation Encroachment,* Santa Monica, Calif.: RAND Corporation, MG-612-OSD, 2007. As of

October 20, 2015:
http://www.rand.org/pubs/monographs/MG612

Lachman, Beth E., Agnes Gereben Schaefer, Nidhi Kalra, Scott Hassell, Kim Curry Hall, Aimee E. Curtright, and David E. Mosher, *Key Trends That Will Shape Army Installations of Tomorrow*, Santa Monica, Calif.: RAND Corporation, MG-1255-A, 2013. As of October 20, 2015:
http://www.rand.org/pubs/monographs/MG1255

Loomis, John B., and Robert Richardson, "Economic Values of the U.S. Wilderness System: Research Evidence to Date and Questions for the Future," *International Journal of Wilderness*, Vol. 7, No. 1, 2001. As of August 31, 2015:
http://www.wilderness.net/library/documents/loomis1.pdf

MacQuarrie, Brian, "Officials Want It to Stay Nomans Land," *Boston Globe,* July 12, 2010. As of August 31, 2015:
http://www.boston.com/news/local/massachusetts/articles/2010/07/12/officials_want_secluded_island_to_remain_no_mans_land/

McCarter, Molly, *Florida Keys Wilderness: A Report on Wilderness Character Monitoring*, U.S. Fish and Wildlife Service: National Key Deer, Key West, and Great White Heron National Wildlife Refuges, August 2012. As of August 31, 2015:
http://ecos.fws.gov/ServCatFiles/reference/holding/23069?accessType=DOWNLOAD

Nellis Air Force Base, "Exercises and Flight Operations," undated. As of August 30, 2015:
http://www.nellis.af.mil/library/flyingoperations.asp

———, *Legislative Environmental Impact Statement for the Renewal of the Nellis Air Force Range Land Withdrawal,* March 1999.

———, *Final Integrated Natural Resources Management Plan, Nellis Air Force Base/Creech Air Force Base/Nevada Test and Training Range*, Nellis Air Force Base, Nev.: 99th Civil Engineering Squadron, Environmental Management Flight, Plan 126-4, February 2010. As of August 30, 2015:
http://www.nellis.af.mil/shared/media/document/AFD-130327-464.pdf

———, *Nevada Test and Training Range Comprehensive Range Plan,* Nellis Air Force Base, Nev.: 98th Range Wing, June 26, 2009.

———, *Nevada Test and Training Range Comprehensive Range Plan,* Nellis Air Force Base, Nev.: 98th Range Wing, January 2011.Nellis Air Force Base and State of Nevada, *Memorandum of Understanding Between Nellis Air Force Base and the State of Nevada Regarding Stonewall Mountain Bighorn Sheep Management*, July 1997.

Nevada Division of Environmental Protection, *Federal Facility Agreement and Consent Order (FFACO)*, February 2008. As of August 30, 2015: https://ndep.nv.gov/boff/ffaco/198app1.pdf

Outdoor Industry Foundation, "The Active Outdoor Recreation Economy," Boulder, Colo., 2006. As of August 31, 2015: http://www.outdoorindustry.org/images/researchfiles/RecEconomypublic.pdf

Outward Bound, "Intercept for Struggling Youth," undated. As of August 31, 2015: http://www.outwardbound.org/intercept/struggling-youth/

Phillips, Spencer R., *Windfalls for Wilderness: Land Protection and Land Value in the Green Mountains*, doctoral dissertation, Virginia Polytechnic Institute & State University, 2004. As of August 31, 2015: https://vtechworks.lib.vt.edu/handle/10919/26112

Public Law 88-577, Wilderness Act, September 3, 1964.

Public Law 94-579, Federal Land Policy and Management Act, October 21, 1976.

Public Law 103-433, California Desert Protection Act, October 31, 1994.

Public Law 106-65, National Defense Authorization Act for Fiscal Year 2000, October 5, 1999.

Reed-Eckert, Melissa, *Species Assessment for Grizzly (Brown) Bear (Ursus Arctos) in Wyoming,* Cheyenne, Wyo.: Bureau of Land Management Wyoming State Office, September 2004. As of August 31, 2015: http://www.blm.gov/pgdata/etc/medialib/blm/wy/wildlife/animal-assessmnts.Par.48642.File.dat/GrizzlyBear.pdf

Robison, Jennifer, "Dream of Coyote Springs Development Still Years Away from Reality," *Las Vegas Review-Journal*, October 26, 2013. As of August 30, 2015: http://www.reviewjournal.com/business/dream-coyote-springs-development-still-years-away-reality

Roosevelt, Franklin D., "Establishing the Desert Game Range in Nevada," Executive Order 7373, May 20, 1936. As of August 30, 2015: http://www.presidency.ucsb.edu/ws/?pid=61181

Rudzitis, Gundars, and Harley E. Johansen, "How Important is Wilderness? Results from a United States Survey," *Environmental Management*, Volume 15, No. 2, 1991. As of August 31, 2015: http://link.springer.com/article/10.1007%2FBF02393853

"S 1338: Military Lands Withdrawal Act of 1999," Congress.gov. As of August 31, 2015: https://www.congress.gov/bill/106th-congress/senate-bill/1338=

Schofield, Roger, "Bullet Background Paper on DNWR Wilderness Study Area, Nevada Test and Training Range/XPN," internal NTTR staff paper, March 27, 2012.

Shenandoah National Park, "Wilderness," undated. As of August 31, 2015: http://www.nps.gov/shen/planyourvisit/wilderness.htm

Sibthorp, Jim, Nathan Furman, Karen Paisley, and John Gookin, , "Long-term Impacts Attributed to Participation in Adventure Education: Preliminary Findings from NOLS," *Research in Outdoor Education*, Volume 9, 2008. As of August 31, 2015: http://www.health.utah.edu/parks-recreation-tourism/docs/nols/sibthorproe.pdf

Stegner, Wallace, "Wilderness Letter," to David E. Peterson of the Outdoor Recreation Resources Review Commission, Berkeley, Calif., December 3, 1960. As of August 31, 2015: http://wilderness.org/bios/former-council-members/wallace-stegner

Taylor, Laura O., Xiangping Liu and Timothy L. Hamilton, "Amenity Values of Proximity to National Wildlife Refuges," Raleigh, N.C.: North Carolina State University Center for Environmental and Resource Economic Policy, April 2012. As of August 31, 2015: http://www.fws.gov/economics/Discussion%20Papers/2012.4.NWRSAmenityReportApril2012withCovers8.pdf

Ten Towns Great Swamp Watershed Management Committee, "Great Swamp Watershed Water Quality Monitoring Report," March 2, 2007. As of September 7, 2015: http://www.tentowns.org/10t/standstu.htm

Teton Science Schools, "Teton Science Schools connects people, nature and place through education, science and stewardship," undated. As of August 31, 2015: http://www.tetonscience.org/index.cfm?id=home

Turner, Monica G., *Fire, Vegetation and Ecosystem Processes in Yellowstone National Park*, Madison, Wisc.: University of Wisconsin Department of Zoology, Ecosystem and Landscape Ecology Lab, undated. As of August 31, 2015: http://landscape.zoology.wisc.edu/Projects/YNP_overview.html

University of Montana Department of Forestry and Conservation, Wilderness.net, "Badlands Wilderness," undated. As of August 31, 2015: http://www.wilderness.net/NWPS/wildView?WID=24

———, "Death Valley Wilderness," undated. As of August 30, 2015: http://www.wilderness.net/NWPS/wildView?WID=151

———, "Delamar Mountains Wilderness," undated. As of August 31, 2015: http://www.wilderness.net/NWPS/wildView?WID=665

———, "Golden Trout Wilderness," undated. As of August 31, 2015: http://www.wilderness.net/NWPS/wildView?WID=210

———, "How Wilderness Benefits You," undated. As of August 31, 2015: http://www.wilderness.net/NWPS/values

———, "Land Classifications Related to Wilderness," undated. As of August 31, 2015: http://www.wilderness.net/NWPS/landClassifications

———, "Number Of Wilderness Units By State (States with most units listed first)," last updated May 29, 2015. As of August 31, 2015: http://www.wilderness.net/NWPS/chartResults?chartType=UnitsByStateMost

———, "Piute Mountains Wilderness," undated. As of August 31, 2015: http://www.wilderness.net/NWPS/wildView?WID=464

———, "The Beginnings of the National Wilderness Preservation System," undated. As of August 31, 2015: http://www.wilderness.net/NWPS/fastfacts

———, "Wilderness.Net's Cabeza Prieta Wilderness Fact Sheet," undated. As of August 30, 2015: https://www.wilderness.net/printFactSheet.cfm?WID=90

———, "Wilderness Acreage By State (States with most acreage listed first)," last updated May 29, 2015: http://www.wilderness.net/NWPS/chartResults?chartType=AcreageByStateMost

———, "Yosemite Wilderness," undated. As of August 31, 2015: http://www.wilderness.net/NWPS/wildView?WID=662

U.S. Bureau of Land Management, *Aravaipa Canyon: Wilderness Management Plan*, July 2013. As of August 31, 2015: http://www.blm.gov/az/st/en/prog/blm_special_areas/wildareas/aravaipa.html

———, "Frequently Asked Questions: The Wilderness Idea," January 2012. As of August 31, 2015: http://www.blm.gov/wo/st/en/prog/blm_special_areas/NLCS/wilderness2/Wilderness_FAQ.html

———, "Muddy Mountains Wilderness," fact sheet, undated. As of August 31, 2015: http://www.blm.gov/pgdata/etc/medialib/blm/nv/field_offices/las_vegas_field_office/wilderness/wilderness_fact_sheet.Par.94163.File.dat/Muddy%20Mountains%20Wilderness%20Fact%20Sheet%20Web%20Opt.pdf

———, *Record of Decision for the Approved Nevada Test and Training Range Resource Management and Final Environmental Impact Statement*, Las Vegas, Nev.: BLM Las Vegas Field Office, July 2004.

———, "Wilderness Study Areas," updated April 3, 2013. As of August 31, 2015: http://www.blm.gov/ut/st/en/prog/blm_special_areas/wilderness_study_areas.html

U.S. Code of Federal Regulations, Title 43, Part 2300, Land Withdrawals, October 1, 2010.

U.S. Defense Nuclear Facilities Safety Board, "Nevada National Security Site," undated. As of August 30, 2015: http://www.dnfsb.gov/about/where-we-work/doe-defense-nuclear-facilities/nevada-national-security-site

U.S. Department of the Air Force, *Air Force Instruction 13-201, Airspace Management*, Washington, D.C.: Secretary of the Air Force, August 21, 2012.

———, *Air Force Instruction 13-212, Volume 1, Nellis AFB Addendum A, Range Planning and Operations*, Nellis Air Force Base, Nev.: Commander 99th Air Base Wing, FOR OFFICIAL USE ONLY, August 1, 2012.

———, *Land Use Study of the Nellis Air Force Range*, Nellis Air Force Base, Nev., September 1998.

U.S. Department of the Air Force and U.S. Department of the Interior, "Memorandum of Understanding Between the U.S. Air Force, Air Combat Command, and the Department of the Interior, U.S, Fish and Wildlife Service," 1997.

———, "Memorandum of Understanding Between the U.S. Air Force, Air Combat Command, and the Department of the Interior, U.S. Fish and Wildlife Service," draft, September 26, 2013.

———, "Memorandum of Understanding Between the U.S. Air Force, Air Combat Command, and the Department of the Interior, U.S. Fish and Wildlife Service," January 23, 2014.

U.S. Department of the Air Force and State of Nevada, "Memorandum of Understanding Between Nellis Air Force Base and the State of Nevada Regarding Stonewall Mountain Bighorn Sheep Management," July 1997.

U.S. Department of Defense, "Department of Defense Press Briefing by Secretary Hagel and Adm. Winnefeld from the Pentagon," Washington, D.C.: Office of the Assistant Secretary of Defense (Public Affairs), July 31, 2013.

———, *DoD Directive 3200.11, Major Range and Test Facility Base (MRTFB)*, December 27, 2007. As of August 30, 2015: http://www.dtic.mil/whs/directives/corres/pdf/320011p.pdf

U.S. Department of Energy, *Final Site-Wide Environmental Impact Statement for the Continued Operation of the Department of Energy/National Nuclear Security Administration Nevada National Security Site and Off-site Locations in the State of Nevada (NNWS SWEIS)*,

Washington D.C.: Office of National Environmental Policy Act (NEPA) Policy and Compliance, DOE/EIS-0426, February 2013. As of August 30, 2015: http://energy.gov/nepa/downloads/eis-0426-final-environmental-impact-statement

U.S. Department of the Interior, "Secretary Jewell Issues Decision on Izembek National Wildlife Refuge Land Exchange and Road Proposal," news release, December 23, 2013. As of August 30, 2015: http://www.doi.gov/news/pressreleases/secretary-jewell-issues-decision-on-izembek-national-wildlife-refuge-land-exchange-and-road-proposal.cfm

U.S. Federal Aviation Administration, *FAA Aeronautical Information Manual*. As of August 30, 2015: http://www.faa.gov/air_traffic/publications/atpubs/aim/aim0304.html#aim0304.html.2

U.S. Fish and Wildlife Service, *2011 National Survey of Fishing, Hunting and Wildlife-Associated Recreation,* September 2013. As of August 31, 2015: https://www.census.gov/prod/2012pubs/fhw11-nat.pdf

———, *Desert National Wildlife Refuge Complex Ash Meadows, Desert, Moapa Valley, and Pahranagat National Wildlife Refuges: Final Comprehensive Conservation Plan and Environmental Impact Statement*, Sacramento, Calif: U.S. Fish and Wildlife Service Pacific Southwest Region, August, 2009. As of August 30, 2015: http://www.fws.gov/uploadedFiles/CCP%20Vol%202.pdf

———, "National Wildlife Refuge System Mission Statement," July 11, 2014. As of August 31, 2015: http://www.fws.gov/refuges/about/mission.html

———, "National Wildlife Refuge System Overview," fact sheet, April 2013. As of August 31, 2015: http://www.fws.gov/refuges/about/faq.html

———, "National Wildlife Refuge System: Permit Applications," March 2013. As of August 31, 2015: https://www.fws.gov/refuges/AirQuality/permits.html

———, *Nomans Island National Wildlife Refuge Final Comprehensive Conservation Plan*, September 2010. As of August 31, 2015: http://www.fws.gov/northeast/planning/nomansland/pdf/finalccp/EntireDocument_LowResolutionforWebPosting.pdf

———, *Rose Atoll National Wildlife Refuge Draft Comprehensive Conservation Plan and Environmental Assessment*, undated.